Rock Climbing in Northern England

Also by Bill Birkett

Winter Climbs in the Lake District (joint author, Cicerone Press, 1980 and 1986)
Lakeland's Greatest Pioneers – a hundred years of rock climbing (Robert Hale, 1983)
Classic Rock Climbs in Great Britain (Oxford Illustrated Press, 1986)
Classic Walks in Great Britain (Oxford Illustrated Press, 1987)
A guide to rock climbing in the Lake District (joint author, Constable, 1987)
The Hill Walker's Manual (Oxford Illustrated Press, 1989)
Modern Rock and Ice Climbing (A. & C. Black, 1989)
Classic Rock Climbs in the Lake District (Oxford Illustrated Press, 1989)

Also by John White

Great Langdale (joint author, FRCC rock climbing guide, 1989)

Rock Climbing in Northern England

Bill Birkett and John White

Constable London

First published in Great Britain 1990
by Constable and Company Limited
10 Orange Street London WC2H 7EG
Copyright © 1990 Bill Birkett and John White
Set in Baskerville 9pt by
Rowland Phototypesetting Limited
Bury St Edmunds, Suffolk
Printed in Great Britain by
BAS Printers Limited
Over Wallop, Hampshire

British Library CIP data
Birkett, Bill
    Rock climbing in Northern England
    1. Northern England. Rock climbing
    I. Title   II. White, John
    796.5′223′09427

ISBN 0 09 468040 X

04358790

Contents

Northumberland

Illustrations
All photographs by Bill Birkett and John White

Yorkshire Limestone

North York Moors

Maps

Acknowledgements

Whilst we alone are responsible for this compilation of climbs, we have drawn on the knowledge of many area specialists. To them, and to all who previously documented the great little climbs of Northern England, we are indebted.

B.B.

J.W.

1989

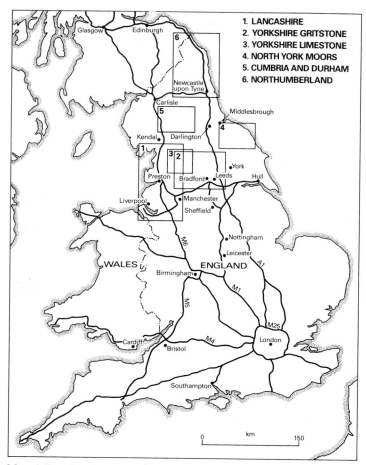

1. LANCASHIRE
2. YORKSHIRE GRITSTONE
3. YORKSHIRE LIMESTONE
4. NORTH YORK MOORS
5. CUMBRIA AND DURHAM
6. NORTHUMBERLAND

Glasgow Edinburgh

Newcastle
upon Tyne

Carlisle
Middlesbrough

Kendal Darlington

York

Preston Bradford Leeds Hull

Liverpool

Manchester

Sheffield

Nottingham

Leicester

WALES ENGLAND

Birmingham

London

Cardiff

Bristol

Southampton

0 km 150

Map delineating the climbing areas

Introduction

For a long time now, following the massive rise in free-climbing standards, and a period of intense rock-climbing development, there has been a need for an up-to-date selective guide to the climbs of Northern England. The Constable series of rock-climbing guides already covers the best from the Peak and the Lake Districts, but the superb climbs of Yorkshire, Northumberland, Lancashire and Durham have never before been collected into one book. By selecting the best from each of these areas, we have produced a collection of superb climbs of wide variety, including many that are arguably the finest gritstone, limestone and sandstone climbs to be found in Britain. Some of the routes are graded at the highest standard of difficulty, but there are enough other climbs here to satisfy all abilities.

It is our belief that a single picture is worth many words, and this guide has been designed to give a highly visual representation of the climbs. The many photographs form the heart of the description and should be used in conjunction with the text to determine quickly and accurately the line of any particular climb.

Climbing is chiefly about personal enjoyment. It doesn't matter just how you climb, or how hard you climb, so long as your actions do not affect the enjoyment of others. Respect the crags and the ethics of any particular area, and look after the environment in which the climbs are situated.

This rock-climbing guidebook is the product of our many years' combined experience on Northern England crags – its compilation was always a labour of love. Should you reap as much enjoyment in using it as we did in compiling it, we will have been rewarded handsomely.

Good climbing!

B.B.
J.W.
November 1988

Notes on the use of the guide

Areas

This guide is split into six distinct regions: Lancashire, Yorkshire Gritstone, Yorkshire Limestone, North York Moors, Cumbria/ Durham and Northumberland. An overall map of Northern England illustrates their juxtaposition. Within these areas each crag has been detailed and an area map shows the location of individual crags. The character of each area is first briefly summarized and then the crags within that area are detailed in alphabetical order.

The climbs

For each major crag there is a photograph with the lines of the climbs clearly indicated. Each climb is specifically referenced to the crag, and to the photograph, by the following system:

BD 1 **Main Wall Eliminate**   14m   E1   5b   *

Line 1, drawn on the crag photograph captioned BD (which is the reference for Bowden Doors in Northumberland), is the line of the route Main Wall Eliminate. *Note:* there may be more than one photograph depicting any particular crag, but all photographs of that crag have the same crag caption reference, e.g. BD for Bowden Doors. When multiple crag photographs do occur, the individual route number identifies the relevant photograph.

If the crag is particularly complex, consisting of separate widely spaced buttresses, then a sketch plan is also used to detail the area. Brimham Rocks in the Yorkshire Gritstone section is an example of this.

Occasionally a line depicted on the photograph, along with the route's name, length, grade and star-rating, is all the information the climber requires to select, locate and climb that route successfully. If this is the case, no further description of the climb is given than, for example, this route on Kyloe-in-the-Wood crag in Northumberland:

KW 17 **Crack of Gloom**   12m   MVS   4c   **

Grades

The usual system of British grading has been used and includes both the overall grade and the technical grade (only when it is 4b or higher) for each pitch. The table below shows typical inter-relationships between overall and technical grades; however, it should be noted that there are always exceptions to the rule. If a route, for example, is particularly serious and sustained, it may have a high overall grade but a technical grade lower than that indicated in the table; conversely, if the route is particularly short, the technical grade may be much higher than the overall grade would suggest.

GRADING TABLE SHOWING BRITISH OVERALL GRADE AND
CORRESPONDING TECHNICAL (PITCH) GRADE

Used Together		
British Overall Grade		British Technical Grade
Moderate		1a
Difficult		2a
Very Difficult		2b
Severe (Mild)		2c, 3a
Severe		3a, 3b
Severe (Hard)		3b, 3c
Very Severe (Mild)		4a, 4b
Very Severe		4b, 4c
Very Severe (Hard)		4c, 5a
Extremely Severe	E1	5a, 5b
	E2	5b, 5c
	E3	5c, 6a
	E4	6a, 6b
	E5	6a, 6b
	E6	6b, 6c
	E7	6c, 7a
	E8	7b, 7c

The increasing international popularity of free rock-climbing and the tremendous rise in the standards of difficulty mean that many will wish to know just how the British grades compare with those used elsewhere. Because of the nature of the British system (consisting of both an overall grade and an individual pitch technical grade) only the pure technical grade can be accurately compared and this is done overleaf:

COMPARISON OF INTERNATIONAL GRADING SYSTEMS

Britain	USA	France	Australia	East Germany	UIAA
moderate	5.2	1		I	I
difficult	5.3	2	11	II	II
very difficult	5.4	3	12	III	III
4a	5.5	4	13	IV	IV±
4b	5.6	5	14	V	V−
4c	5.7	5+	15	VI	V
5a	5.8	6a / 6a+	16	VIIa	V+
5b	5.9		17	VIIb	VI−
5c	5.10a	6b / 6b+	18	VIIc	VI
5c	5.10b				
	5.10c	6c / 6c+	19	VIIIa	VI+
6a	5.10d		20	VIIIb	VII−
6b	5.11a / 5.11b / 5.11c	7a / 7a+	21	VIIIc	VII
6c	5.11d	7b / 7b+	22	IXa	VII+
	5.12a		23	IXb	VIII−
7a	5.12b	7c / 7c+	24	IXc	VIII
	5.12c	8a / 8a+	25	Xa	VIII+
	5.12d		26	Xb	IX− / IX
	5.13a	8b / 8b+	27	Xc	IX+
7b	5.13b	8c	28		X−
	5.13c		29		X
	5.13d		30		X+
	5.14a		31		
			32		
			33		

Systems

The British method of grading rock-climbing is unique. A detailed explanation is given in *Modern Rock and Ice Climbing* by Bill Birkett, but for the purposes of this guidebook the combined experience of both authors and a consensus of opinion among many others have been used to arrive at the grades given. For the first time a consistent standard of grading has been applied to the whole area, though it is impossible to remove all 'local flavour' from any particular area because of the vastly different types of climbing to be found. In Northumberland, for instance, there are many climbs on the undercut short sandstone cliffs that are extremely technical to start but then become much easier. Therefore it may first appear that the technical grade outweighs the overall grade – the climber, however, tackling these routes will soon appreciate the grading allotted. Grades given allow for perfect conditions and for climbers using all the modern equipment in standard use.

Star rating

All the routes included in this selected guide are worthy climbs. However, for those who wish to be even more selective the following star rating has been adopted:

* good   ** very good   *** excellent

Again this has been standardized to a high degree but each rating should also be related to the individual crag on which the climb occurs.

Access and conservation

At both a national and an international level we are at last becoming more aware that we must look after our environment. The issues which cause concern range from global topics such as the destruction of the great rain-forests and the effects of CFCs on the ozone layer down to local litter clearance and tree-planting schemes. It is in everyone's interest that climbers as a group consider very carefully their actions in relation to the environment. There is a limited amount of rock suitable for climbing on in this country – we cannot create another Malham or Bowden Doors – and actions which alter the rock will remain for ever. The chipped holds and bolt holes cannot be repaired; they leave permanent scars. It is our hope that in the search for ever harder routes on diminishing rock supplies, climbers do not deny future generations their chance to explore genuinely untouched rock. If you can't do it, leave it for someone else who can; do not bring it down to your own level. The Yorkshire crags have suffered more than any from hold-chipping and bolt-placing. Although the bolting of routes at places like Malham has led to big increases in standards and a number of immensely enjoyable routes, it is worth considering how future generations will view these actions. Hold-chipping is inexcusable and it is sad that, at the time of writing, it seems to be a growing disease in many areas. It must not be allowed to continue.

· Looking after the crags goes much further than this. Many of the areas described have special characteristics to consider, such as the valuable flora on and around many of the Yorkshire limestone cliffs, and the recolonization of some crags by rare nesting birds such as peregrines. Instead of setting out a long list of *do*s and *don't*s, we suggest that climbers aim to follow just one rule from the Country Code: *Respect the life of the countryside.* Keep the crags clean, learn something about the wildlife with which you share the crag and climb in harmony with nature. Consider every form of wildlife encountered as valuable and keep your effect on it to a minimum. Watch out for special considerations in the introductions to each crag and respect the views of ornithologists and botanists, who share our enthusiasm for the crags. In any case, the Wildlife and Countryside Act is very much on their side and it would be wise not to risk any confrontation which could damage either the reputation of climbers as a group or the freedom to climb on any particular crag.

There is unrestricted access to many of the crags described in this guide, but access to others has certain conditions attached. Some of the Yorkshire crags, for example, are not approachable on public rights of way, and landowners have requested that permission to climb be asked, or certain access routes used. The British

Mountaineering Council, through its area committees, has worked very hard to secure agreements which suit all parties, and it is in everyone's interest that they are adhered to. Details, where appropriate, have been given in the introduction to each crag. If problems are encountered, treat the situation with tact and contact the Access and Conservation Officer at the BMC.

Note: The inclusion of any crag in this guide is no indication that there is either a right of access or a right to climb upon it.

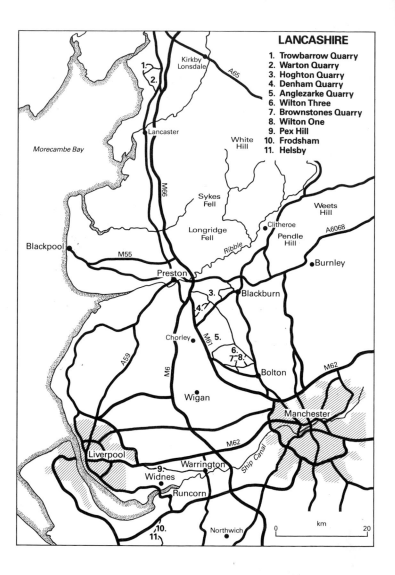

LANCASHIRE

1. Trowbarrow Quarry
2. Warton Quarry
3. Hoghton Quarry
4. Denham Quarry
5. Anglezarke Quarry
6. Wilton Three
7. Brownstones Quarry
8. Wilton One
9. Pex Hill
10. Frodsham
11. Helsby

Lancashire

Strictly speaking, with the inclusion of Helsby, Frodsham and Pex Hill, this section extends a little beyond the Lancashire boundary. However, all the climbing has an undeniable 'Lancs' – red rose county – feel to it. As many of the climbs are found on the quarried rocks in or near the industrial towns and cities of the North, they provide a perfect release for the city-based climber and are ideal for a short day or an evening.

There are many excellent routes, some very demanding, on the three main rock groups of the area – the sandstones, grits and limestone – each of which provides its own particular form of entertainment. The area covered is a large one, stretching from Warton and the Cumbrian border in the north down to Helsby and the Cheshire plain in the south.

Anglezarke Quarry   GR SD 621162

Situation and access
This sunken quarry is situated above the reservoirs on Anglezarke Moor, just off the M61 near Winter Hill. Accessible and sheltered, it is justifiably popular. From Junction 6 on the M61 take the A6027 to the A673 Bolton to Horwich road. Turn left along this until, 1 mile past Horwich, a right turn is made by the Millstone Inn. This road leads to a motorway bridge but turn right immediately before the bridge is reached to continue along to the Yew Tree Inn. The right fork here is taken and the road leads across the reservoir (via a bridge) where a turn left leads to the entrance (signed) of a large car-park/picnic area (a concrete road leads steeply up to this). Park at the far end of this and take the tracks which lead out across the road over a wooden fence on to the rim of the extensive quarry. The easy scramble descent is obvious and placed centrally (2 minutes).

Character
The rock is a soft type of grit and although it offers positive flake
holds, care should be exercised. The quarry is roughly rectangular
with the main (longest) walls described facing approximately west
and east, and therefore some sunshine and dry rock can usually be
found.

The climbs
From the top of the approach bank overlooking the quarry the areas
and climbs are described from far right to left, working in an
anticlockwise direction.

Grey Buttress

AZ 1 **Years from Now**   9m   E2   5c   *

AZ 2 **Whittacker's Almanac**   8m   HS

AZ 3 **Sheppey**   17m   E2   5c

AZ 4 **Storm**   17m   VS   4c   **

AZ 5 **Kaibab**   17m   E1   5b

AZ 6 **Elder Groove**   17m   MVS   4b

The next area on the left is known as Coal Measure Crag
because of the black shale band above it. It tends to weep for
some while after wet weather and is not described here. Left
again is a distinct prow of rock, the most handsome in the
quarry – this is the Golden Tower area.
Golden Tower Area
The descent lies on the buttress to the right.

AZ(1–6), Anglezarke Quarry, Grey
Buttress

AZ (7–11)

AZ(7–11), Anglezarke Quarry,
Golden Tower area (left)

AZ(8), Golden Tower, Anglezarke
Quarry (right)

AZ 7 **Samarkand** 20m VS 4c **
This is the corner crack bounding the right side of the tower.

AZ 8 **The Golden Tower** 24m E2 5c ***
A Lancashire classic giving sustained climbing in the upper
section. Start from a small recess on the left edge of the tower
and climb the crack to exit right on to the ledge in the centre
of the face. The finishing crack directly above is well
protected but never easy.

AZ 9 **Please Lock Me Away** 17m E5 6b *
The undercut flake (crux) leads to the thin crackline. This is
then followed to the top.

AZ 10 **Klondyke** 17m E4 6a *
The crack – care should be taken with the rock in places.

AZ(12–23), Anglezarke Quarry, Left Wall area

The next route described lies on a wall approximately 25m left of here – Falkland Wall.

Falkland Wall

AZ 11 **Tangerine Trip**   17m   E3   6a   **

A steep sustained route with a certain compulsive attraction. Starts approximately centrally and follows the diagonally rightward slanting crack in the reddish wall.

The next routes described are round on the approach face to the left of a broad easy descent break.

Left Wall Area

AZ 12 **Edipol!**   12m   HS   4a

The crack and bulge enable a crack up the wall above to be taken to a ledge. Move right and climb the edge of the wall to finish.

AZ 13 **Terror Cotta**   21m   HVS   5a   ***

The yellow corner is climbed to the ledge. Step left on to the wall and climb on flat holds to the overhangs above. Step

right and up through the bulge via a groove.

AZ 14 **Double Trip**   18m   E2   5b   *
Start midway along the wall and climb past peg runners to
the overhang. Reach a good hold and move up directly
through the overhang.

AZ 15 **First Finale**   18m   E2   5c   *
The thin crack and groove above give steep climbing. Care
should be taken arranging protection.

AZ 16 **Fingertip Control**   15m   E3   6a   *
The start is balancy and is followed by a long reach to reach
a ledge hold. Continue precariously in the same line to the
top. Serious with the hardest moves high up – but good
climbing.

AZ 17 **Many Happy Returns**   15m   HVS   5a
The crack in the middle of the wall.

AZ 18 **Metamorphosis**   17m   VS   4c   **
From the right arete move up to reach the top of the flake.
Continue directly to a small ledge then slightly right to
finish.

AZ 19 Punchline   15m   HVS   5a

Near the left end of the wall is an obvious little niche. Move up the wall until level with the porthole then move right to it. Finish to the left.

AZ 20 Telegraph Arete   9m   MVS   4b

AZ 21 Shorty   9m   E1   5b

The weakness about 2m left of the arete leads leftwards first to a mantelshelf right and then a direct finish.

AZ 22 Wedge   9m   HS   4a

The steep crack left of the corner.

AZ 23 Nightmare   8m   MVS   4b

The inverted Y-crack.

The scrambling descent and usual point of entry on first arrival to the quarry lie just to the left of this cracked wall.

BQ(1), Brownstones Quarry

BQ(2), The lads in Brownstones Quarry

Brownstones Quarry   GR SD 681125

Situation and access
This quarry is found just off the small moorland road (known as
Scout Road) that links the A675 at Wilton to the B6226 at Bob's
Smithy. Just over a mile out of Wilton there is a row of cottages
(Old Colliers Row) and entrance to the quarry is by the end of these
(2 minutes). There is ample parking opposite the cottages.

Character
A favourite bouldering area. There are good problems of all grades
which never exceed 9m in height.

The climbs
Individual description is unnecessary – just follow the chalk.

DQ (1–7)

Denham Quarry   GR SD 592228

Situation and access

This quarry lies close to the junction between the M6 and the M61.
Approach from Junction 29 on the M6 and follow the A6 south for a
mile to a small roundabout at Clayton Green. Turn left here and
another roundabout is reached after half a mile. Turn left, cross the
motorway (M61) and a short way further turn right into Holt Lane
and continue until the quarry is reached on the left. Parking is
possible in the quarry itself.

Character

An open quarry with some excellent routes, normally on good rock,
though there are the usual distractions of this sort of area such as
litter, graffiti and motor cycles.

The climbs

The routes described are on the larger buttress on the right of the
quarry, near the pool, and are described from left to right.

DQ 1 **Splash Arete**   11m   VD   **

    Climb on to some big ledges right of the pool and move left
    to an exposed finish up the arete. A good route at its grade.

DQ 2 **Flick of the Wrist**   19m   E1   5b   *

    Gain the arete and climb directly to the bulge. Surmounting
    this is not easy. Finish up Complete Streaker.

DQ 3 **End of Time**   22m   E1   5b   *

    Start on the large ledge and mantel on to a small ledge up on
    the right. Continue rightwards to the break and overcome
    the bulge on the left of the cave on good holds, to a direct
    finish.

DQ(1–7), Denham Quarry

DQ 4 **Time** 22m HVS 5a
Start as for the last route but move slightly left and up to the break. Climb diagonally up to the right into a vague scoop and trend right above this to finish.

DQ 5 **Complete Streaker** 29m VS 4c ***
Climb the left slanting gangway to the break. Traverse this rightwards almost to the arete and cross the roof to a ledge. Finish direct from the left side of this. Exposed and quite serious, a good introduction to top end VS climbing.

DQ 6 **Timepiece** 27m HVS 5a
A steep start on pockets leads to a small ledge system. Traverse leftwards past a flake and hand traverse until a crack just round the arete leads to the top.

DQ 7 **Mohammed The Mad Monk of Moorside Home for Mental Misfits** 16m VS 4c **
An excellent route whose name does it an injustice. Hereafter known as Mohammed. The eye-catching, right slanting groove on the left of the buttress gives a sustained route which is never too hard and always enjoyable.

Frodsham   GR SJ 520765

Situation and access
Situated a short way out of Frodsham on the wooded west flank of Frodsham Hill, these steep little buttresses are easily accessible. Head south out of Frodsham along the A56. A road on the left (B5393) leads off to Tarvin and in less than a mile there is a farm on the right. There is limited parking on the verge here – don't block

DQ, Denham Quarry, Mohammed. The Mad Monk

FS (1-3)

any gates. Just past the farm on the left a private road leads up the
hill to join the woods. At this point continue directly up the hillside
on the obvious path (large private house on the right). This veers
left near the top of the hill to reach the first overhanging buttress –
Hoop-la Buttress (15 minutes). There is a distinct horizontal track
running along the top edge of the hill just above all the individual
buttresses. This serves as the easiest means of access to the different
areas but only if their locations are known – if in doubt contour
along the edge from beneath Hoop-la Buttress.

Character
Although short, the buttresses are usually overhanging and the
routes, on soft red sandstone (beware of holds snapping), are full of
character! Treated as a bouldering area, although some routes are
best lead roped, the area gives excellent value and there are some
problematical and strenuous climbs. The setting, high in the woods
overlooking the plain below, is pleasant, and the rock generally
clean and attractive.

The climbs
There are several distinct buttresses stretching from Hoop-la on the
right end to Great Wall on the left end. All have numerous problems
and the lines are very obvious. With the exception of Great Wall the
climbs rarely exceed 8m in length and separate description is
unnecessary. However there are three readily identified roof
problems on Hoop-la Buttress and these are famous enough to merit
separate description from left to right.

Hoop-la Buttress

FS 1 **The Hoop-la**   5m   5b
>The central crack splitting the main overhang. A diagonal
>line of holds leads to the crack on the lip of the roof.

FS(1–3), Frodsham, Hoop-la Buttress

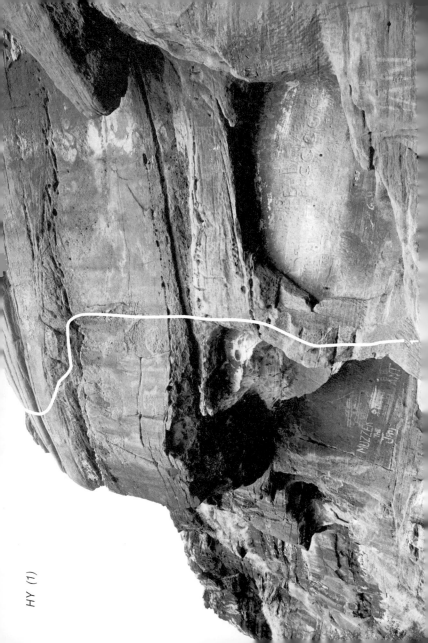

HY (1)

FS 2 **Boysen's Route**   5m   5c

About 2m right of the last route – a horizontal break and pockets lead to a hold below the lip. Use this then pull through the gap between the flakes.

FS 3 **Banner's Route**   5c

Start about 2m right again to climb the right edge of the overhang.

All three are good value and the other buttresses yield many more which are similar – very strenuous!

Helsby   GR SJ 518750

Situation and access
Readily seen from the M56 this crag is perched on the hill directly above Helsby village. A road from the village passes under the end of the crag (limited parking on the verge). Where the road reaches the wood a steep sandy path leads directly up through the trees to the right end of the crag (5 minutes).

Character
Once an extremely popular crag, with a keen local following (in addition to those dropping in on their way to or from Wales), it is no longer so attractive. One reason for this is the extensive green lichen skin thought to be propagated by the nearby chemical works. However, while this is undoubtedly a problem, there are still clean areas offering worthwhile and varied climbing. The rock, soft red sandstone, should be treated with caution but is generally good on the routes selected.

The climbs
The routes are described from right to left. For the most part there is

HY(1), Helsby, West Buttress

an upper tier, of black-looking rock, but only the obvious bottom wall of West Buttress is included here. Much else remains, with almost 150 routes recorded, but a wire brush is advised should one wish to venture further.

The West Buttress

HY 1 **Eliminate 1**   15m   E1   5b   ***
Climb the pillar to the right of the overhang and continue up the wall to the spikes. Traverse left to a knob and then move directly to the top with an awkward mantelshelf.

HY 2 **Flake Crack**   12m   VS   5a   ***
Friend protection now makes this a steady proposition.

HY 3 **Twin Caves Crack**   12m   S   4a

HY 4 **Dinnerplate Crack**   11m   HS   4b

HY 5 **Greenteeth Crack**   9m   D   *
A good chimney climb.

HY 6 **Greenteeth Gully**   9m   M
This can be used as a means of descent to all the routes described.

The first half of the wall immediately to the left of Greenteeth Gully is not dealt with here but the climbs on its left end are described, commencing just past a small birch tree.

HY 7 **Little by Little**   9m   S   4a   **
Scramble up the ledges to climb the wall on pockets to reach a mantelshelf. Move up right to a leftward leaning corner and pull up this using a finishing hold on the right.

HY(2–4), Helsby, West Buttress

HY(8), Grooved Slab, Helsby (above)

HY(4–6), Helsby, West Buttress (right)

HY 8 **Grooved Slab**   11m   HS   4a   ***
  The groove leads to a mantelshelf. Move left to gain the
  central groove and climb it to exit right or left. Fine delicate
  climbing.

HY 9 **The Twin Scoops**   11m   E1   5b

HY (7–10)

10

← base
obscured.

8

9

HY 10 **The Beatnik**   12m   E5   6a   **
> The shallow groove in the wall leads to the left end of the distinct oblique overhang. Reach the overhang to step right then pull up directly. Finish via a chimney to the left. Both strenuous and delicate, this is Al Rouse's famous test-piece.
>
> Unfortunately the wall to the left is extremely green and Morgue Slab (E1 5c), pulling through the cave midway along (utilizing a drill hole for the finger above the cave), will most likely require wire brushing prior to making an ascent. Much more rock remains to the left but no more routes are described.

Hoghton Quarry   GR SD 626265

Situation and access
Its proximity to Blackburn, Preston and Blackpool makes this an important climbing ground. A large quarry cut from the wooded hillside below Hoghton Tower, it unfortunately tends to have a generally northern aspect. It is situated in private grounds and there have occasionally been access problems which seem, at the time of writing, to have been resolved by the BMC. There is a notice before the entry to the quarry displaying the agreed restrictions and these should be strictly observed. The quarry lies on the A675 between Preston and Blackburn. When proceeding from Preston the Boar's Head pub is reached (on the left) before Hoghton Tower and the road along its side – Chapel Lane – is taken until a railway bridge is crossed. There is limited parking on the verge outside the Wesleyan Chapel but do not block the track leading down right immediately after the bridge or the farm entrance. Take the track which leads down parallel with the railway line, through a gate to the railway crossing point. Cross the railway line here (take care, this is a main line double track) and then turn left following a path which leads to

HY(7–10), Helsby, left side of West Buttress

PH, Pex Hill,
Lady Jane Direct (left)

HTQ(1–2), Hoghton Quarry,
Hoghton Wall (right)

a muddy cutting and then the quarry with the Hoghton Wall
immediately on the right.

Character
This is the highest and most extensive quarry in the area.
Unfortunately it doesn't see much sunshine and because of the
extensive tree cover it can retain a damp green atmosphere for some
time. Additionally the rock, a soft grit, requires care, and a sandy
soil can be washed down from the top and from ledges when it rains.
But there is no denying the verticality and striking nature of many of
the lines – there are some very good routes here.

The climbs
The layout is simple enough and basically consists of a continuous
series of walls beginning, on the right, immediately on entering the
quarry. The routes are described from right to left.

HTQ (1–12)

1

2

HTQ (3-4)

4

3

Hoghton Wall

HTQ 1 **The Wasp** 24m HVS 5a **
The corner leads to an exit right on a ledge.

HTQ 2 **Boadicea** 37m E2 5c
The thin crack and then the wall above.

HTQ 3 **Route One** 35m VS 4b *
Take the crack and continue to the ledge. Up a corner until
a mantelshelf gives access to a series of ledges leading
rightwards to the block overhang. Take this on the left and
continue directly to the top.

HTQ 4 **Mandarin** 37m E2 5b ***
Bold and undercut climbing provides a route of substantial
character. Follow the corner and short wall to the large roof.
Traverse rightwards into the hanging groove in the nose and
up to an overhang. Pass this on the right and continue into a
niche. Exit by pulling out left around the arete and finish up
the easier ground to the top.

The wall now indents – Main Amphitheatre – but the next
area described is the high square-cut tower over to the left.

Rhododendron Buttress

HTQ 5 **Rhododendron Buttress** 18m E2 5c **
Gain the corner and continue to the ledge. Take the line of
least resistance to the left end of the overhang above. Over
this using the crack and continue to the sandy band of rock.
Step left and up to the top (the left crack is easiest).

HTQ(3–4), Hoghton Quarry, Hoghton Wall

HTQ (5–6)

HTQ 6 Cave Route 43m S
    Start as for the previous route.
    1. 15m. The slab leads to the corner groove then up to the ledge. Traverse out left to belay in the corner.
    2. 15m. Traverse left until the arete is rounded, move up and then left to a large ledge.
    3. 13m. Continue up the corner to a dirty ledge on the right. Continue up the crack overlooking the corner to the top.

    No further routes are described on this wall but opposite, across a sump below, there is a shorter wall which is more open and does get the sunshine. Reach it by continuing round to the left until easy ground leads round the sump to its base.

    Liqueur Wall

HTQ 7 **Creme de Menthe** 15m VS 4b

HTQ 8 **Curacao** 17m E2 5c

HTQ 9 **The Effect of Alcohol** 18m E2 5c

HTQ 10 **Kummel** 17m S

HTQ 11 **Benedictine** 15m E1 5b *

HTQ 12 **Maraschino** 15m E3 6a *

HTQ 13 **Tia Maria** 15m VS 4c

HTQ 14 **Goldwasser** 18m VS 4b *

HTQ(5–6), Hoghton Quarry, Rhododendron Buttress

HTQ(7–14), Hoghton Quarry, Liqueur Wall

HTQ (7–14)

Pex Hill   GR SJ 501887

Situation and access
This is the North-west's secret weapon, offering unparalleled
outdoor training and bouldering within the region. Cut into the flat
top of a hill this hole in the ground was once used as a reservoir.
Today the clean-cut vertical walls provide a quick-drying and
sheltered climbing ground of the highest quality. It is situated some
3 miles north of Widnes near the village of Cronton. On the M62
from Manchester take Junction 7 and follow the A569 towards
Widnes then turn right along the A5080 towards Liverpool. Just
before entering the village of Cronton turn right to follow an
unsurfaced track to park by the iron railings immediately above the
quarry (Dateline wall). On the M62 from Liverpool take Junction 6
and then follow the A5080 towards Widnes. Go through Cronton to
turn left on to the track as described above.

Character
The sandstone is excellent, hard and full of tiny pebbles which
provide the finger and toe holds. The short routes, generally around
8m, are always good value and with something like 130 individual
routes recorded (not including the many traverses and combinations)
the technical difficulty rarely falls below 5b and is most often above
this. Fingery and technical, the short vertical walls are sheltered and
dry quickly, offering a bouldering ground *par excellence*.

The climbs
The quarry consists of numerous interesting walls, the longest being
that immediately right (looking back out of the quarry) of the
entrance. The lines are mostly obvious and well chalked and
individual description is unnecessary. An exception to this could be
made of the wall immediately under the car-parking area where it is
usual to lead Dateline. Therefore two climbs on this wall will be
described from left to right.

PH(1–2), Pex Hill, Dateline Wall

PH 1 **Dateline** 12m E2 5c ***

PH 2 **Black Magic** 12m E5 6b ***

Trowbarrow Quarry GR SD 481758

Situation and access

Located near Silverdale, a few miles north of the Carnforth junction (J35) on the M6, Trowbarrow is a conveniently sited and justly popular disused limestone quarry. On the road from Silverdale station towards Yealand Redmayne, Leighton Moss Nature Reserve first appears on the right and then in a couple of miles, just as the road leaves the wood to descend a steep little hill, a path will be observed leading up the tree-covered bank on the left. There is ample parking on the verge at this point. Follow the path, which leads in a few hundred yards into the quarry. Proceed along the length of the quarry with the first buttress appearing on the right (5 minutes). Occasionally there have been access problems, although these appear to be resolved at the time of writing. However, should the quarry owners ask you to leave, then please do so courteously.

Character

This is a pleasant place to climb but care must be taken with the rock. The Main Wall is actually detached from the mother rock behind, due to blasting, and the striking crack climbs are stress fractures – it is quite conceivable that the whole wall may at some stage collapse. In addition, the face is formed from a matrix of fossils which tend to snap off with little warning. However, despite continual rumours of its imminent collapse, the wall has stood with little change for many climbing years. On the opposite side of the quarry to the Main Wall, hidden in the trees, the overhanging Red Wall forms a favourite top-roping ground for wet days.

The climbs

The first buttresses occur on the right and the routes are described in anticlockwise manner from right to left.

On the right the descent path can be easily identified running down to the bank on the quarry floor. Below and left of this is a little buttress and left again a broken-looking overhanging white wall.

TB 1 **Square Deal Surf**   14m   VS   4c

About 3m left of the edge of the buttress there is a ledge at 2m height. From this climb the wall on the right to another ledge. Move left to gain and follow twin cracks to the top.

TB 2 **Biological Agent K9**   14m   HVS   5a   *

The wall and thin crack above.

TB 3 **First Cut**   9m   D

The corner crack above shot hole 156.

Yellow Wall

The routes here are rather muddy but give worthwhile climbing when dry.

TB 4 **Willy the Disk**   18m   HVS   5a

The cracks direct starting 3m right of shot mark 155.05.

TB 5 **Earth Eater**   18m   VS   4c

Directly above shot mark 155.05 but move right to finish.

TB 6 **Street Boy Blues**   23m   E1

Gain the parallel cracks and continue to the bulge moving round this taking the diagonal crack. Easier climbing up the wall finishes the climb.

Main Wall

TB (7-16)

TB 7 **Warspite** 27m E1 5a *
Take the big corner to a horizontal break 3m below the final
roof. Gain the left edge of the wall and continue left along
the horizontal crack to gain the wide vertical crack. Take
this to the top.

TB 8 **Warspite Direct** 27m E2 5b **

TB 9 **Hollow Earth** 29m E1 5a **
A good but rather gripping route.

TB 10 **Touch of Class** 29m E1 5a ***
Intimidating but excellent climbing – the potential dangers
are obvious.

TB 11 **Jean Jeanie** 30m VS 4c ***
A tremendous route at the top of its grade. The hardest
section occurs midway when transferring right.

TB 12 **Aladdinsane** 29m HVS 5a ***
The overhang leads to an awkwardly wide crack – another
fine climb.

TB 13 **Cracked Actor** 33m E2 5c ***
Move left from Aladdinsane after the first 9m to follow the
obvious crack which curves up the wall. An excellent climb
but care should be taken with all the holds on the wall.

TB 14 **Red Slab** 21m VS 4b

TB 15 **Original Route** 37m D *

TB 16 **Carling's Wall** 12m E5 6a
An extremely serious lead due to the brittle nature of the
fossil holds.

TB(7–16), Trowbarrow Quarry, Main Wall

TB (17–24)

TB 17 **Pigfall**   24m   S

TB 18 **Jomo**   34m   D   *

Assagai Wall

The large wall on the left with notable fluted drainpipes at its tops.

TB 19 **Assagai**   38m   HVS   5a   ***
The grotty groove leads to a left traverse beneath the overhang. The wall is then climbed direct to a brilliant finish up the fluted drainpipe.

TB 20 **Sleeping Sickness**   32m   E2   5c   *
A sustained climb which is high in the grade.

TB 21 **A Sense of Doubt**   18m   E5   6a
A contrived route forcing its way up the blank wall. Three poor knife blades, and other dubiously placed protection, once protected the bottom of the wall but most of this is now dangerous or missing and the route receives few, if any, leads.

Over to the left there is one narrow clean slabby wall before the end wall of the quarry.

TB 22 **Barrier Reef**   21m   S
The rib right of the wall.

TB 23 **Coral Sea**   21m   VS   **
Start up the rib, as for Barrier Reef, but after a few metres move left to climb the centre of the slabby wall via series of cracks.

TB(17–24), Trowbarrow Quarry, Assagai Wall

TB 24 **Coral Sea Direct Start**   6b   *

An excellent and baffling problem start leads directly up the slabby wall.

Red Wall

This is the overhanging wall of curious rock immediately opposite Main Wall. Hidden by trees, it takes some considerable time to get unclimbably wet. The climbing is intense with generally no protection and progress is made on rounded polished holds and clay-filled pockets. Some of the routes have been led but the norm is to top rope the routes from the conveniently sited trees above.

Izzy the Push E3 5c is the most obvious shallow groove on the right of the wall and there are another dozen routes all of which are harder.

The Warton Area

The fell on which the Warton crags are situated can be clearly seen from the M6 and is dominated by the huge, broken-looking main quarry.

Warton Main Quarry   GR SD 492144

Situation and access
The huge quarry which is visible to the west of the M6. Leave the motorway at the Carnforth turning and locate the Black Bull in the centre of Warton village. Turn off the main road by this pub and drive up a gentle hill for about one mile to an obvious gate on the right which leads into the quarry.

TB(19), Assagai

Character

Although the quarry is very disappointing on initial viewing, the far end contains some excellent routes which can only be seen adequately from that end, due to the way the quarry walls face. The rock is often good on the routes described, but loose and potentially dangerous areas will be encountered and steadiness and experience are useful virtues here.

The climbs

At the opposite end of the quarry to the entrance are a number of long grooves separated by slabby areas. One such slab, to the left, has an attention-grabbing thin crack splitting it.

WQ 1 **The Third World** 45m HVS 4c ***
> Start by scrambling up to the foot of the aforementioned crack. Climb the crack, which is highly enjoyable and well protected until it merges into a corner. Avoiding some hanging blocks, gain cracks on the left which lead steeply to the top. A gem.

WQ 2 **Deceptive Bends** 45m E1 5a ***
> Start as for the last route. Climb the crack for about 9m and place a runner. Descend to a delicate traverse line which leads to the right-hand arete. Up this to a mediocre peg runner and a thread a little higher. Move up and right to a roof (good runners at last) and move over its left-hand end to a peg. A short wall with good holds leads to some easy scrambling. Delightful slab climbing providing answers just when they are required, but still bold and sustained.

WQ 3 **The Real World** 46m VS 4c

WQ 4 **Plastic Iceberg** 48m E1 4c 5b *
> The stark groove on the right of this area of rock.

WQ, Warton Quarry, Deceptive Bends

1. 23m 4c. Climb rather loose and broken rock to the foot of the groove.

2. 25m 5b. The groove is sustained and a shaky traverse right at its top leads to a welcome end.

Other Warton Crags

Warton Small Quarry (GR SD 498724) lies adjacent to the car-park on the right a short distance up the road from the Black Bull. Plenty of short routes and some traversing on rock as smooth as the glasses in the pub.

There are two crags up on the fell above the small quarry. The Upper Crag (GR SD 494728) can be seen on the very top of the hill; Warton Pinnacle Crag (GR SD 492727) is lower than this and to the left in a wooded area. Both can be approached from the back of the small quarry or from parking areas on the road before the main quarry. The routes are short but good.

Wilton One   GR SD 699134

Situation and access
The quarry is situated directly behind the Wilton Arms, a pub just outside Bolton on the A675 Bolton to Preston road. There is a car-park in addition to the pub car-park. A steep bank guards the entrance to the quarry but once this is breached the back (east-facing) wall is more or less continuous from bottom left to top right.

Character
In truth Wilton One could never be described as aesthetically inspiring. The soft grit shines green when the walls are wet and the view is obscured by the bank opposite the quarry face. Nevertheless

WQ(1–4), Warton Quarry

W1(1–5), Wilton One, The Allotment area

it is a convenient place to climb for many and, as it is long and fairly high, there are numerous climbs worthy of attention.

The climbs
The routes are described from left to right.

The Allotment

W1 1 **Puma** 14m E2 5c
Twin cracks lead to a break. Step left, ascend the overhang and up to the top.

W1 2 **Flimnap the Pirate** 9m VS 4c

W1 3 **First Cut** 14m HVS 5a
Move up to a large pocket – peg runner – then directly up the wall.

W1 4 **Green Wall** 15m VS 4b

Up to a pocket then move right to a corner scoop and follow
this to a horizontal break. Move right to finish up left.

W1 5 **Jean** 15m VS 4c

The groove can be reached directly or by traversing in from
the left. It leads to the horizontal fault then take the broken
corner on the right.

The Pitface

This is the stretch of more broken rock and no routes are
detailed here.

Chimney Buttress

W1 6 **Leucocyte Left Hand** 18m E3 6a

W1(6–13), Wilton One, Chimney Buttress and Outside Face of the Prow

W1 7 **Leucocyte Right Hand** 18m VS 4c *

W1 8 **Central Route** 18m E1 5b **

W1 9 **Wombat Chimney** 20m E1 5b *
The flared chimney.

W1 10 **Loopy** 14m E4 6a
A pillar of rock is gained directly and climbed on its left.

Outside Face of the Prow

W1 11 **Fingernail** 21m S **
There is an iron hook in the rock: gain this, climbing from

the right or left, then move left for 2m before climbing up again to a ledge. Go diagonally rightwards to a weakness and climb it.

W1 12 **Flingle Bunt**   20m   VS   4c
The crux is entering the shallow top groove above the ledge.

W1 13 **Cameo**   18m   E1   5a   **
Not much in the way of protection.

Inside Face of the Prow

Possibly the cleanest area of rock in the quarry.

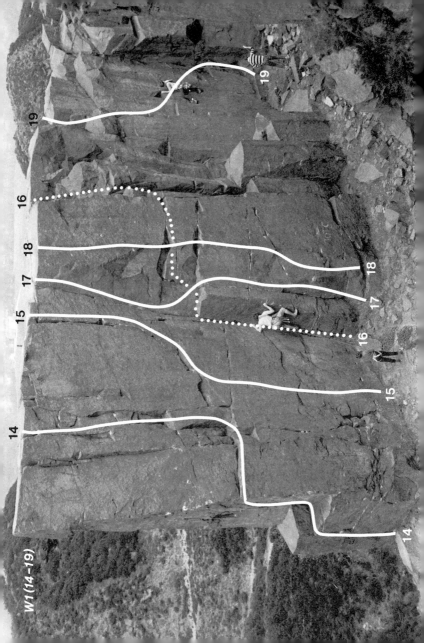

W1 (14-19)

W1 14 **Dawn** 14m E1 5b **
> The crack to the right of the edge starts the route.

W1 15 **Innominate** 14m E3 6b

W1 16 **Eliminate** 18m MVS 4b *
> The corner groove is taken to a ledge – once this is gained
> hand traverse right to reach the top.

W1 17 **Ann** 14m E1 5b *
> The thin crack to the ledge and then the layback crack to the
> top.

W1 18 **Cheat** 14m E2 5c

W1 19 **Flywalk** 12m HS *
> Holds lead left from the corner and then a crack through the
> overhang is followed. A classic problem is to start directly –
> 5c.

> The largest and highest section of the quarry begins to the
> right of here but most of the routes are generally harder,
> slower-drying, rather vegetated and dirty in the cracks – care
> should also be taken with the rock. Anyone wishing to climb
> here is therefore left to their own salvation.

Wilton Three   GR SD 695135

Situation and access
Not far along the A675 Bolton to Preston road, just past the Wilton
Arms pub, a road breaks off up the hill to the left – this is known as
Scout Road. Near the top of the hill, some way before the bend,
there is a gate on the right (ample parking) with a track leading

W1(14–19), Wilton One, Inside Face of the Prow

W1(17), Ann, Inside Face of the Prow, Wilton One

steeply up into a quarry – Wilton Three (2 minutes). Wilton Two (containing a shooting range) and Wilton Four (very small) are the quarries further up the hill.

Character
This is the friendliest and quickest-drying of the Wilton quarries with a good selection of routes, There is a shooting butt in the quarry but this does not appear to be in regular use at the time of writing.

The climbs
The routes are described from left to right.

Orange Wall

W3 1 **Great Chimney**   8m   M

W3 2 **Orange Wall**   9m   VS
A number of variations exist.

W3 3 **Orange Crack**   8m   HS   4a
The left crack of the pedestal.

W3 4 **Justine**   6m   S
The right side of the pedestal.

W3 5 **Orange Groove**   9m   VD

W3 6 **Monolithic Crack**   8m   VS   4b

W3 7 **Cedric**   8m   S

W3 8 **Orange Corner**   8m   HVD

Constable's Overhang Area

W3 9 **Oak Tree Wall**   9m   S

W3 10 **Tea Leaf**   8m   VS   4b

W3 11 **Oak Leaf Crack**   9m   D

W3 12 **Forked Cracks**   9m   VS   4b
The right crack of the inverted Y.

W3 13 **Parallel Cracks**   11m   S

W3 14 **The Groove**   11m   HVD   *

W3(1–21), Wilton Three, Orange Wall and Constable's Overhang area

W3 15 **Slime Chimney** 12m VD

W3 16 **The Grader** 14m E3 6a **
Take the crack out of Slime Chimney.

W3 17 **Thunder** 14m HVS 5a

W3 18 **Constable's Overhang** 14m E4 6b ***
The peg-scarred crack leads to a ledge. Move right and take
the crack through the overhang.

W3 19 **Nameless Edge** 12m HVS 5a

W3 20 **Central Crack** 11m HVS 5a **

W3 21 **Crack and Slab** 9m VD **
The ledge can be gained by a variety of starts. Once gained
climb on to a block and take the short crack above.

Waterfall Buttress

W3 22 **Foot Corner**   11m   VS   4b

W3 23 **Canine Crucifixion**   12m   E1
Climb the crack just right of the arete to finish on the right
up a short corner.

W3 24 **Brastium**   12m   E1   5b
The steep crack is often a watercourse.

W3 25 **Betty's Wall**   12m   E1   5a   *

Rappel Wall Area

W3 26 **Barbecue**   14m   S

W3 27 **Rappel Wall**   17m   VD   **

W3(22–31), Wilton Three, Waterfall Buttress and Rappel Wall Area

W3 28 **Shiver's Arete**   14m   E1   5b   *
   The hardest bit is at the top.

W3 29 **Canopy**   14m   HVS   5a   *
   The corner leads to a crack.

W3 30 **Kay** 14m VS 4b **

W3 31 **Crooked Crack** 12m VS 4c *

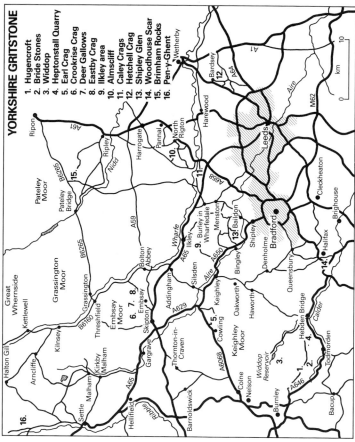

YORKSHIRE GRITSTONE

1. Hugencroft
2. Bride Stones
3. Widdop
4. Heptonstall Quarry
5. Earl Crag
6. Crookrise Crag
7. Deer Gallows
8. Eastby Crag
9. Ilkley area
10. Almscliff
11. Caley Crags
12. Hetchell Crag
13. Shipley Glen
14. Woodhouse Scar
15. Brimham Rocks
16. Pen-y-Ghent

Yorkshire Gritstone

Yorkshire

Yorkshire is a large county of great contrasts. The industrial towns of what used to be the West Riding give easy access to remote moorland and quiet dales. The crags, too, are varied. They are split into two sections, Limestone and Gritstone, which works well from the point of view of both rock type and geography. Most of the limestone crags lie within the Yorkshire Dales National Park and they are found exclusively north of Skipton. The gritstone outcrops are mostly south and west of this area, often within easy reach of the major towns. There is everything here for the climber, from well-bolted mega-desperates to protectionless slabs and brilliant bouldering areas. There are sheltered crags, routes that remain dry even in heavy rain, and exposed, remote situations with magnificent outlooks and a high mountain feel. The weather is typically varied, but it is normally possible to climb all year round, especially using winter sun traps such as Malham, and in any case conditions are generally better than in neighbouring areas to the north and west. There is good beer in profusion – Tetley, Timothy Taylor and Theakston to name a few – and a plentiful supply of excellent food at the right price, from the curry houses in Bradford to the more conventional fish and chip shops. A climber's paradise!

Gritstone

Almscliff Crag   GR SE 268490

Situation and access
One mile north of the main Harrogate to Otley road, about 5 miles out of Harrogate, Almscliff is situated in an elevated and exposed position amidst pleasant farmland. The best approach is via the village of North Rigton along Crag Lane. The best parking is at the north-west end of the crag – be careful not to block any entrances

AC (1-8)

and avoid parking next to the farm. A short walk up the fields
(access via a stone stile) leads to the crag.

Character
A very fine crag, Almscliff is tough and uncompromising. The routes
tend to be strenuous and proficiency in using rounded holds and in
jamming is an asset – as are big arms! There are however a number
of delicate and technical routes for those who don't spend the winter
bulking up in the gym. The rock is finest gritstone and provides the
usual friction, though the more popular routes and boulder
problems are becoming increasingly polished. The crag dries quickly
and it is often possible to find a sheltered place even though the crag
is notoriously windy. At the time of writing there have been
problems associated with the use of the land around the crag as a
grazing area, and the ensuing and inevitable mess. A small towel
may be found useful! There are classic routes of all grades here, and
unparalleled bouldering. There are two main parts to the crag –
Low Man and High Man – along with many beautiful boulders.
High Man has four faces: north-west, west, south-west and south.

The climbs

Low Man

Described from right to left.

AC 1 **Kiernan's Traverse and Rough Crack**   9m   S

AC 2 **Stew Pot**   11m   VD
Start below a circular hole. Up and past this to finish via a
short crack.

AC(1–8), Almscliff Crag, Low Man

AC 3 Low Man Easy Way   12m   M

AC 4 Fluted Columns   14m   VD   **
Sloping ledges lead to the flutes. Climb these on good holds
and leave them rather boldly for the grade.

AC 5 Whiskey Wall   12m   E3   5c

AC 6 Square Chimney and Whiskey Crack   14m   S   **
A fine combination. Climb the cleft to an awkward exit on
the right and tackle the steep crack which provides some
embarrassingly good jams and a welcome finish.

AC 7 Piggot's Stride   8m   HS
Bridging across from the Matterhorn Boulder feels scary.

AC 8 V Chimney and Traverse   13m   VD   *
A polished chimney opposite the Matterhorn Boulder gives
access to a good traverse under the small roof. The direct
finish over the roof is an awkward VS.

High Man
The climbs are described from right to left, starting right of
the stone wall which meets the south-west face. The first
routes are on the Black Wall, at whose foot is an often
uninviting landing.

AC 9 Black Wall   11m   VS   4c

AC 9a Black Wall Eliminate   9m   E2   5c   *
Stand on the large flake (easier said than done), traverse left
to a slim crack and aim up for the next break and move left
again to a crack that splits the final steep section.

AC, Almscliff Crag, Whiskey Crack

AC (9a–17)

AC 10 **Birdlime Direct**   E3   6a

AC 11 **Birdlime Traverse**   E1   5b   **
> Climb via a glossy ramp and a nose to meet the traverse line. Along this, moving down a little at one point to meet the Eliminate. Right again to finish up a steep little wall. The start of the Eliminate and a reverse of the traverse give a good climb.

AC 12 **South Face Climb**   13m   S

AC 13 **South Chimney**   11m   VD

> There are some good problems immediately left and right of the chimney.

AC 14 **Yellow Wall**   13m   E2   5c   *
> A leftwards traverse under the big roof out of South Chimney. Thought-provoking.

AC 15 **South Chimney Layback**   13m   S
> An attractive little climb starting up the thin hands jam crack before moving right to finish up the arete right of the chimney.

AC 16 **Shuffle Crack**   13m   E1   5c
> One of those routes best described as a classic of its type.

AC 17 **China Syndrome**   14m   E5   6c   *

> The next routes lie left of the stone wall.

AC 18 **Stomach Traverse**   11m   VS   5a
> Better than the name suggests. A strenuous start leads to better holds and a finish up easier angled rock.

AC(9a–17), Almscliff Crag, High Man, South Face

AC (18–25)

AC 19 **Central Crack**   11m   S

The undercut wall to the left has some crucial problems.

The Crucifix takes the crack just left of the arete, whilst the line on or just right of the arete is harder. Much harder is the wall to the right of here – Pebble Wall, a very frustrating 6b.

AC 20 **Three Chockstones Chimney**   10m   M
A good descent.

AC 21 **Demon Wall**   10m   HVS   5b   ***
Start up the chimney and traverse quickly out to the wall on the left. Typical gritstone break climbing leads to a puzzling finish.

AC 22 **Bird's Nest Crack**   10m   S   ***
The conspicuous and highly polished crack is a good jamming test. A variation start to the right gains the original route near 'the bit that sticks out'. Good and slightly harder.

AC 23 **The Traditional Climb**   10m   VS   4c   **
The next crackline to the left. The secure jams have to be abandoned in the central section.

AC 24 **Pothole Direct**   10m   VS   5a

AC 25 **The Pothole**   10m   VD

A wide break, The Rift, separates the south-west face from the north-west face. On its north side, the Tight Chimney (Moderate) can be a problem for the stouter person despite its lowly grade.

AC(18–25), Almscliff Crag, High Man, South-west Face

AC (26–31)

AC 26 **Oublette**   9m   E2   5c   *
Left of the chimney is a steep break containing some pockets.
Traverse in from the right, climb the break with difficulty
and exit right. Neat.

The West Face

Round to the left from The Rift is a huge roof, under which
are The Goblin's Eyes.

AC 27 **The Goblin**   11m   VD
A typical Almscliff VD, climbing past the eyes and sidling
left to finish up the chimney.

AC 28 **Orchrist (The Goblin's Roof)**   11m   E4   6b   ***
An incredible route taking a wild line through the centre of
the roof. The fun does not end at the lip. More than one
belayer is pretty much essential.

AC 29 **The Zig-zag**   11m   VD

AC 30 **Zig-zag Direct**   9m   VS   4c

AC 31 **The Nose**   9m   VD
The hardest V Diff in the world.

Lots of problems in this area, including the brilliant Syrett's
Roof, which takes the overhang left of Zig-zag.

North-west Face

The first route lies down to the left from a chimney.

AC(26–31), Almscliff Crag, High Man, West Face

AC (32–42)

32, 36, 49

32, 33

34

37

33, 34

Girdle traverse

35, 37

35, 36

38

39

40

41

AC 32 **Crack of Doom**   VS   4c   **
: The impressive corner crack leads to the roof. Traverse right on improving holds to an easy finish.

AC 33 **Great Western**   HVS   5a   ***
: The same corner crack, but this time a leftwards traverse under the roof. Gain a well-earned rest on a pinnacle and finish straight up the crack, or the one to the right. Exposed and very classic. A direct finish over the roof from the initial crack, via pockets is Grand Illusion E3 5c.

AC 34 **Western Front**   14m   E3   5c   ***
: Climbs directly and strenuously up cracks in a small roof to join Great Western at the pinnacle.

AC 35 **Wall of Horrors**   16m   E3   6b   ***
: Mega-classic. Start left of The Niche at a well-worn wall with an undercut base. A big jug a few metres up seems a long way away. Climb to and pull over the roof above, with a precarious move to end up with feet ensconced in the break. Work right and then back left to an exit.

AC 36 **All Quiet**   27m   E4   6b   **
: A sustained traverse links the break on The Wall with Crack of Doom.

AC 37 **The Emms Telegram**   17m   E4   6a

AC 38 **Long Chimney**   16m   D   **
: An excellent beginner's chimney with a slightly harder finish which comes out left near the top.

AC(32–42), Almscliff Crag, High Man, North-west Face

AC (43–49)

Parson's chimney

Girdle traverse

43

44, 49

44

45

46

47

48

49

Left of here is a detached pinnacle, The Pulpit. Left again is a striking corner crack, whose right wall is often emerald green.

AC 39 **Frankland's Green Crack**   14m   VS   4c   **

Climb the crack, move right and enter the upper crack with some difficulty. A route of sustained interest.

AC 40 **The Big Greeny**   14m   E4   6a   *

The wall left of the last route with a difficult upper section, easily recognized by a conspicuous pocket.

AC 41 **Parson's Chimney**   16m   HS   ***

A classic in the traditional style. A strenuous start leads to exciting and exposed climbing with finishing holds guaranteed to produce a smile.

AC 42 **Overhanging Groove**   16m   VS   4c   **

The flake and shallow crack/groove left of the chimney give an excellent route.

AC 43 **Central Climb**   14m   HS   *

A crack system taking the easiest line up the centre of the lower wall. Good jamming technique will be useful.

AC 44 **Z Climb**   14m   VS   4c

AC 45 **Why Climb**   10m   E2   5c

The steep wall left of the last climb, reached via a neat little problem known as the Teaspoon Variation, which succumbs to a decisive approach.

AC(43–49), Almscliff Crag, High Man North-west Face

51 →

50

AC 46 Cup and Saucer 13m Diff *

A varied climb taking the left side of the cave via some weird moves to a big chockstone. The left wall provides a fitting finish.

AC 47 Encore 9m E2 5c *

Start beneath some overhangs round to the left of the last route where an easy angled slab goes from left to right. Climb to a large flake and move left to a break in the roof, which is climbed somewhat gymnastically.

AC 48 Finale Slab 13m HVS 5a

From about half-way up the easy slab, climb to the roof and take a delicate leftwards traverse which leads to a short finishing crack.

AC 49 The North-west Girdle 61m HVS 5a ***

Though girdles are not that popular on grit, this one's a must. From the start of Z Climb's top leftwards traverse, go right to Central Climb, step down and make a hand traverse into Parson's Chimney. Up rightwards, round the corner and another hand traverse leads to Frankland's. Gain The Pulpit and either do the splits or make yet another hand traverse to Long Chimney, which is climbed to a belay near its top. Move round beneath a roof to cross Wall of Horrors and reach Great Western's pinnacle. Reverse this route to join the traverse of Crack of Doom. A sustained, exposed and strenuous outing.

Boulders

Problems of all standards are to be found in this bouldering mecca, along with hundreds of variations. Just go out and have a good time! One boulder is especially worthy of

AC(50–51), Almscliff Crag, The Virgin Boulder

mention, as the problems are of a length which nudges them up into the route category.

The Virgin Boulder

The huge block to the left of Low Man, with a particularly steep lower side.

AC 50 **The Gypsy** E2 6a *
The awesome right-hand arete of the lower face. Technical and strenuous, and the hard bit arrives just when you thought victory was in sight.

AC 51 **The Virgin** E2 6b *
Start at the left end of the wall and follow the evil horizontal break to where desperate moves gain shallow pockets and a pinch before the final mantel.

Opus E4 6b is the face just right of the Gypsy arete, while the left arete of the overhanging face is the The Lady 6c. The rear of the boulder has some routes to suit more gentle tastes.

Brimham Rocks GR SE 209637

Situation and access
The rocks lie on a high plateau of land a few miles east of Pateley Bridge and a couple of miles north of the B6165. The rocks are a well-frequented tourist attraction and are signed from this road. The National Trust owns most of the rocks, but some of the routes are still on private land, so climb with courtesy. Parking is either in the main car-park which is administered by the Trust and on which a charge may be made, or on one of the smaller areas on the perimeter road.

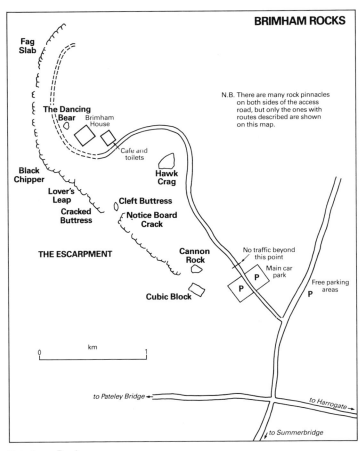

BRIMHAM ROCKS

Fag Slab

The Dancing Bear

Brimham House

Cafe and toilets

Black Chipper

Hawk Crag

Lover's Leap

Cleft Buttress

Cracked Buttress

Notice Board Crack

THE ESCARPMENT

Cannon Rock

No traffic beyond this point

Main car park

P

P

Free parking areas

P

Cubic Block

N.B. There are many rock pinnacles on both sides of the access road, but only the ones with routes described are shown on this map.

km
0   1

to Pateley Bridge ←

to Harrogate →

to Summerbridge

Brimham Rocks

Character

Wind and water have left their mark at Brimham in the shape of hundreds of uniquely eroded pinnacles and towers. These and the surrounding escarpments are composed of a coarse Millstone Grit which provides friendly friction at the expense of some horrifying skin-shredding potential. The routes are normally steep with rounded holds and fierce jams, but some excellent slabs exist also. In poor weather, some parts attain a green sheen very rapidly, but there are always clean areas as well as acres of bouldering. Due to the dispersed nature of the various climbing areas, readers might find it useful to use the map in conjunction with the descriptions and a little imagination!

The climbs

Cubic Block

This is the closest area to the main car-park. Exit from the top left-hand corner of the left-hand car-park over a small rise to the huge tilted block. The routes are described in an anticlockwise fashion, starting at the left-hand arete of the slab.

BR 1 **Old Corner**   9m   MS

BR 2 **Heather Wall**   11m   S
Start a few metres right of the left arete and gain a sloping ledge by a few problem moves. Climb the crack on the right to the top. (Descent is via a large jammed boulder on the left and a small subsidiary crag.)

BR 3 **Great Slab**   11m   S

BR(1–4), Brimham Rocks, Cubic Block

BR(5–6), Brimham Rocks, Cubic Block

BR 4 **Cubic Corner** 11m HS **
The right-hand arete of the block. Good, with the crux in a
high and serious position.

BR 5 **Stone Wall** 13m E1 5b

BR 6 **Rough Wall** 13m VS 5a *
Round to the right is a steeper slab which contains a thin
crack splitting a tiny roof high up on the right. Pleasant
climbing up the breaks leads to the crack, a comforting
runner and the crux. Around the corner again is an
impressive overhanging wall.

BR 7 **Joker's Wall** 12m E3 6a ***
The depressingly steep left-hand side of the wall. Start at a
posse of underclingable pockets. Powerfully up to the next

holds and undercling once more to gain good holds. Traverse right, move up and either finish up a short jam crack or traverse back left to a desperate grovel.

BR 8 **Minion's Way** 11m VS 5a **

The widening crack splitting the centre of the wall. The lower crack is climbed via a frustrating and knuckle-rearranging jam to good holds and a resting ledge. The upper crack is not without interest.

BR 9 **Beatnik** 13m E2 5c

Right of Minion's Way is a cave. On the left of the cave is a broken flake crack. Climb this and then force a way through the rounded bulges to a left trending finish.

Cannon Rock is the next worthwhile feature and lies diagonally back from the edge towards the main track, a few

BR(10–12), Brimham Rocks, Cannon Rock

minutes' walk from Cubic Rock. The descent is by a
reasonable jump on to another block, or by a climbdown
(easier than it looks) at the back of the pinnacle.

BR 10 **Frensis** 11m VS 4c **
The east face contains twin cracks. Ascend these and the
short crack above on a variety of good holds and jams.
Traverse right from the top of the crack to a worrying
finishing mantel which is considerably less secure than the
rest of the route.

BR 11 **Frensis Direct** 11m E1 5b ***
As for Frensis, but continue up the top crack with difficulty.

BR 12 **Maloja** 11m MVS 4b **
Climb a short scoop left of Frensis to some flutings. If you're
feeling the pinch at this point, continue up and then left to a

BR(13–15), Brimham Rocks, Noticeboard Crack area

hole from where the top is easily reached. Pleasant, with a well-defined crux.

Moving back down to the escarpment, the southern side of a gap has a wall with one of Brimham's best-known routes.

BR 13 **Noticeboard Crack**   9m   VS   4c   *
Ascend the crack, which is both too wide and too narrow for comfort.

BR 14 **Noticeboard Wall**   9m   E2   5c

BR 15 **Buena Ventura**   11m   HVS   5b

Cleft Buttress lies across the gap and slightly towards Brimham House.

BR(16–17), Brimham Rocks, Cleft Buttress

BR 16 **Lancet Crack** 13m VS 5a *
   A stout climb with some exciting moves.

BR 17 **Cleft Buttress** 13m M
   A good easy route which takes a worn line up a series of
   steps, starting in the cleft.

Cracked Buttress

This is the next good part of the crag encountered down on
the escarpment, recognizable by a fine trio of cracks up a
steep wall.

BR 18 **Cracked Corner**   7m   D

BR 19 **Right-hand Crack**   13m   HS   **
The right-hand crack of the trio has some awkward moves –
a route to get stuck into.

BR 20 **Central Crack**   13m   VS   4b   *

BR 21 **Parallel Cracks**   11m   VS   4c
Reasonable climbing leads to an exit which sees plenty of
grovelling. Left are some rather dirty and broken routes, but
soon a fine clean slab can be seen, which is unfortunately
used a little too much for abseiling.

BR(18–21), Brimham Rocks, Cracked Buttress

R (18–21)

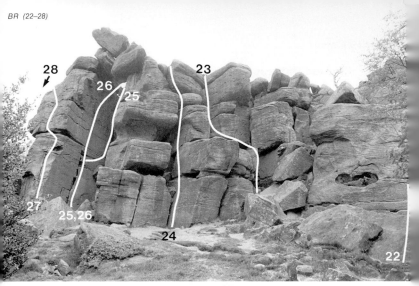

BR(22–28), Brimham Rocks, Lover's Leap area

BR 22 Lichen Slab   8m   VD   *

The middle section of the slab provides a look at harder things for the V Diff leader.

BR 23 President's Progress   9m   VD

BR 24 Nameless Chimney   14m   HS

BR 25 Lover's Leap Chimney   14m   VD   **

A route of great character starting up the polished crack in the left wall of the big recess. From the top of this crack traverse right and ascend the first chimney on adequate holds.

BR 26 Left Wall   16m   E5   6a

A route with few suitors. Continue past the top of the first crack of the previous route up a slender line, before moving right on to the impending wall and finish left of the chockstone.

BR 27 **Birch Tree Wall**   16m   VS   4c   ***
A surprisingly delicate climb of continuous interest. Climb a groove and step right to the arete. Up and back left to a beautiful scoop and gangway. The direct start to the scoop is 6a.

BR 28 **Difficult Crack**   7m   VD
Round the corner to the left from Birch Tree Wall is a crack with a conspicuous jammed boulder. Climb past this to a bridging finish.

A couple of cricket wicket lengths further along is a wall topped by an overhang and containing a flake crack. A good and perplexing VS, White Rose Flake, climbs to the roof and exits right. Another area of bouldery crags is soon reached.

BR 29 **Ritornel**   6m   HVS   5b

BR 30 **Dogleg Crack**   13m   HVS   5b

BR 31 **Rotifer**   8m   E3   6a
The left-hand arete of the bay with some long reaches.

BR 32 **The Arch**   6m   E1   6a   **
A great little climb with a hard boulder problem start leading to a finish through the top of the arch.

The pinnacle to the left of here sports a well-known classic.

BR 33 **The Black Chipper**   13m   E1   5b   **
Climb the wall left of the arete, past a ledge to a thread which gives valuable protection. Trend right to pull out via a

BR(29–33), Brimham Rocks, The Escarpment

chipped hold. Maybe for a few seconds chipping won't seem so bad after all.

The edge resumes play 200m or so further on. Towards the left-hand side of this buttress is a corner topped by a boulder.

BR 34 **Not Rob**   8m   HVS   5c
The front of the arete right of the corner. Technical and harder than it looks.

BR 35 **Great Corner**   9m   D
The corner to the boulder and step right, or slightly harder, the wall to the left.

BR 36 **Gnome's Arete**   10m   MVS   4b

Back right from this area is a short wall with a series of flake holds. This is the line of Duggie's Dilemma, a good Severe. A couple of minutes' walk leads to the Hatter's Groove area.

BR 37 **Hatter's Groove**   13m   HVS   5a   **
An easily seen and clean groove on the right of the buttress. Exit left. The right-hand exit is a similar standard.

BR(34–36), Brimham Rocks, The Escarpment

BR (34–36)

BR(37–41), Brimham Rocks, The Escarpment

BR 38 **Grit Expectations**   E4   5c   *

The wall and groove left of the last climb.

BR 39 **Slippery Crack**   13m   S

Often found in a state befitting the name, when it feels insecure.

BR 40 **Last Crack**   8m   S

BR 41 **Close to the Hedge**   8m   E3   5c

Left is a gully. The wall left of here has a good HVS 5b – The Hattery.

BR 42 Charming Crack 10m E1 5b *

A vicious crack which is certainly not as its name suggests. A good and sustained struggle and not for soft hands. The overhanging crack to the left is:

BR 43 The Brutaliser 10m E3 5c

The name tells you all you need to know.

BR 44 Hanging Groove 8m HVS 5b

BR(42–44), Brimham Rocks, The Escarpment

(42–44)

BR(44–47), Brimham Rocks, The Escarpment

BR 45 **Pig Traverse**   13m   S
Start where a wall runs up to meet the crag. Climb cracks to the break. Traverse right and finish up the arete.

Round the corner are two hard routes.

BR 46 **Gigglin' Crack**   11m   E6   6b
Takes the disgusting-looking off width.

BR 47 **True Grit**   11m   E2   6a   *
Takes the thin hanging crack to the left, with a vicious starting section.

The last section on the escarpment is an attractive and open slabby area with some good easier routes.

BR 48 **Fag End**   8m   MS

BR 49 **Silk Cut**   8m   E2   6a

BR 50 **Fag Slab Variant**   8m   VS   4c

BR 51 **Fag Slab**   8m   S   *

BR 52 **Allan's Crack**   13m   VS   4c   ***
A beautiful layback corner leads to some good moves round
the bulge and a finish back right and up the top slab. A
direct start up the slab is quite possible.

The next section can be easily reached from Brimham
House.

BR(48–52), Brimham Rocks, The Escarpment

BR (55-60)

Hawk Crag

A large blocky pinnacle off to the right from the first bend as one returns from Brimham House to the car-park.

BR 53 **Cakewalk** 9m VS 4c
The crack and difficult wall on the left.

BR 54 **Rainy Day** 15m E1 5c
Start at a bush 5 yards right of Cakewalk. A steep wall and cave, then left and up.

BR 55 **Picnic** 13m E2 5c

BR 56 **Picnic Variation** 13m HVS 5a

BR 57 **Jabberwok** 13m HS *

BR 58 **Swan Arcade** 13m E2 5c *

BR 59 **Desperation Crack** 13m HVS 5a *
The aptly named off width requires top-rate technique or about 10,000 calories.

BR 60 **Hawk Traverse** 22m S

The crack in the wall opposite Desperation Crack is Domesday Crack VS 4c, which is similar in nature.

Caley Crags   GR SE 231444

Situation and access
The crags can be seen on the south side of the A660 Leeds to Otley road, about a mile past the crossroads with the main Bradford to Harrogate road. Parking places exist on the roadside near a gateway which gives access to the crags and to the popular bridleways and footpaths. The roadside boulders lie across to the left from here and the main crag is five minutes' walk up the bridleway to the right.

Character
Easy access and a fantastic selection of boulder problems mean that this is a busy crag, the bouldering probably being more popular than the routes. The crag faces north, with all that implies, but the quality of the rock and good views create an experience which is difficult to beat, especially on a summer's evening.

The climbs

Roadside Buttress and Boulders
These areas are easily reached by turning left at the gateway and gently ascending for a couple of minutes.

There are limitless possibilities here, and new problems seem to appear regularly. The routes described are those whose length takes them beyond a conventional boulder problem, but the greatest joy is probably in the discovery of many others.

Two huge blocks form the longest routes here and a good identifying feature is the overhanging roadside face which has a number of scalloped circular and shallow pockets. Just right of here is a slab split by a classical boot-wide crack.

CC, Caley Crags, Permutation Rib

CC (1–10)

CC 1 Morris Dance VS 5a
The wall just right of the crack, which is:

CC 2 Morris Crack S

CC 3 Hanging Groove E1 5b

CC 4 Rabbit's Paw Wall HVS 5b
A long reach helps to gain easier and attractive climbing.
Round to the left is a corner with attractive slabs either side.

CC 5 Permutation Rib VS 5a
Start just right of the Unfinished Crack, traverse right to the
arete and follow this daintily. Direct up the wall is 5c.

CC 6 Unfinished Crack VS 5a
Secure jams lead to a rather insecure exit.

CC 7 Little Cenotaph VS 4c
The corner crack is a bit of a struggle.

CC 8 Marrow Bone Jelly E6 6c
A hideous name for very hard friction climbing on a wall
which is too steep for friction climbing! Takes the arete to
the left of the corner.

CC 9 Adrenalin Rush E5 6b
The easy crack in the slab is followed by difficult and
puzzling climbing.

CC 10 Psycho E5 6b
Make a difficult step across from a boulder at the left end of
the wall on to a line of chicken heads. Scratch up these. The
direct start is an impossible-looking 6c.

CC(1–10), Caley Crags, Roadside Boulders

CC (12–14)

Boot crack →

12

13

14

Up the hill from here is another steep face with a
conspicuous incomplete flake in its centre. This is:

CC 11   **The Great Flake**   E6   6b

The arete to the right is 7a. The reader might note that no
stars have been given for these routes – they are all excellent
and most of the boulder problems equally so.

The Main Crag
Approach by following the bridlepath up to the right from
the gateway. The first feature reached is the Sugar Loaf
Boulder, on the right of the path, with a companion boulder
just before it on the left.

CC 12   **Angel's Wall**   VS   4c   ***
A short but heavenly route up the steep wall right of the
pathside slab. Dynamic, requiring a confident approach and
finishing all too soon. A bit short for three stars, but so good!

Two good VS's take lines on the opposite side of the boulder,
whilst on its rear are:

CC 13   **Plantation Ridge**   VS   4c   *
The left arete is sustained and requires the gentle touch.

CC 14   **Central Route**   VS   4c
The cracks up the centre of the slab.

A boulder on the opposite side of the path has some good
longer problems and the large block behind and right of this
has a mean-looking off width – Boot Crack HS. The arete to
the left is Black Jumper E1 5b. There are many other
problems near here.

CC(12–14) Caley Crags, Sugar Loaf Boulder

CC (15-31)

The routes on the main crag are described from left to right.

At the left end of the crag, a passageway can be found, between the main edge and a large boulder. The boulder has some good problems.

CC 15 Fingernacker Crack 8m E2 5c *
The trying thin crack and a difficult move into the easier upper crack.

CC 16 Holly Tree Scoop 11m D (the crack exit is VD)

CC 17 Frank Miller 9m E2 5c
The slab, vague crack, and pockets, right of the holly tree.

CC 18 Noonday Ridge 16m E1 5b ***
Start right of the big arete and work left on to a steep wall from the second ledge. Pull into a scoop and climb the slab above. Varied and continuously exciting.

CC 20 High Noon 16m E4 6a ***
Gain the arete from the previous route and climb it sensationally with a swing to the right near the top.

CC 21 Fred Zinnerman 16m E4 6b **
The wall to the right with a very hard move past a bolt.

CC 22 Lad's Corner 14m VS 4c
Start in the recess and climb the left-facing corner. Feels tough. The chimney is Block Chimney VS 4c whilst the oft-looked-at arete to the right is:

CC 23 Amazing Grace 14m E6 6c **

CC(15–31) Caley Crags, Main Crag

The Scoop

32

33

CC(32–33) Caley Crags, Main Crag

CC 24 **Compulsion Crack** 14m VS 4c
The wide crack and chimney to the right.

CC 25 **Forecourt Crawler** 13m E4 6b *
The peg-scarred crack which starts in the little corner to the
right. Wimp out into Compulsion Crack or ascend the steep
wall boldly to a boulder problem in the sky finish.

CC 26 **Pedestal Wall** 18m S *
A good route climbing up the left edge of the big leaning
block and the left side of the wall above via a big pocket to
an exciting finish.

CC 27 **Rib and Slab**   14m   VS   5a
Balancy moves up an arete just to the left of a chimney
(Square Chimney VD) lead to a ledge. Finish up the chipped
wall.

CC 28 **Tipling Crack**   13m   HVS   5a
The crack in the right wall of the chimney, with a testing
upper section.

Round to the right is an attractive pocketed slab.

CC 29 **Tip Off**   8m   E2   5b
Start on the right of the slab by a crack. Gain the break,
traverse left to the slab centre and ascend direct on pockets.

CC 30 **Rip Off**   8m   E2   5c   *
Directly up the blunt arete to the right.

CC 31 **Tipster**   9m   VS   4c
Climb the wide crack to the break, traverse left past the last
two routes and ascend a blunt arete.

Across right again is a handsome buttress.

CC 32 **Quark**   16m   E4   6a   *
The peg-scarred crack and handy arete lead to a bolt, but
only with great difficulty.

CC 33 **Zig Zag**   14m   S   *
Climb steep cracks to a final pleasant jamming traverse
along the diagonal crack. An excellent variation finish is The
Scoop 4c, which goes up to the left where the diagonal crack
goes right.

CR (1–3)

Crookrise Crag   GR SD 987557

Situation and access

These crags are situated high on the moors north of Skipton. The easiest approach is from Embsay village. Take the road leading left out of the village on to the moor. A good car-park is found by the reservoir; do not park higher up the track by the farm. From the car-park, follow the track towards the farm until a good path can be seen leading up the moor and running parallel with a wall to the left. Up this path to where the fell levels off and turn left until a stile leads over the wall and down to the rocks.

Character

Quite a lonely crag with beautiful views and a feel of the wild about it. The rock is top quality grit and the routes are generally clean and sound. A rather special place.

The climbs

The routes are described from right to left. The first feature of the main crag after descending from the access stile is a well-worn slab.

CR 1 **Route 1**   12m   VD

Follow the right-hand edge of the slab to a break. Move left, aiming for a short crack. Up this delicately, finishing up the buttress on the left if desired.

CR 2 **Edge**   8m   S

CR 3 **Route 2**   11m   VS   4c

There are numerous problem starts and some other pleasant slab routes here.

Leftwards is a gully and then a steeper buttress.

CR(1–3) Crookrise Crag

CR(4–6) Crookrise Crag (above)

CR 4 **Twin Cracks**   11m   S

CR 5 **Ledge Buttress**   11m   VS   4c

CR 6 **Tiger Rag**   8m   S   *
Struggle on to a ledge on the left-hand arete of the buttress
and continue up the wall on the left.

CR, Crookrise Crag, Old Lace (left)

CR (7–13)

CR 7 **Chockstone Crack** 8m

CR 8 **Bilberry Crack** 8m   MVS   4b

The next important buttress can be identified by a slab
which leans against its right-hand side.

CR 9 **The Sole** 9m   VS   5a   **
Start at the left-hand arete of the buttress at a thin crack.
Some weird moves up this lead to more conventional
climbing up the leftward slanting crackline. Tough.

CR 10 **Mother's Little Helper** 10m   E1   5b
Start as for the last route then right and up through the
small roofs. Good ropework and modern protection make it a
fair challenge.

CR 11 **West Wall Climb** 7m   VS   4c
Start at an obtuse arete on the wall left of The Sole.
Interesting climbing on mostly rounded but good pockets.

CR 12 **Walker's Wall** 14m   VS   4c
Set back to the left of the last route is a wall topped by a
roof. Start at the arete on the left, move back to the centre of
the wall and go straight through the awesome-looking but
easy-feeling roof

The overhanging wall to the left is:

CR 13 **Longlurch** 8m   E1   5c
Start on the left, swing across right and pull through the
bulges.

CR (14-17)

The next routes are on a slabby buttress recognized by a central crack –

CR 14 **Diagonal Crack** VD – with an undercut slab immediately to its left.

CR 15 **Old Lace** 12m VS 4c *
Traverse left from the bottom of Diagonal Crack for a couple of metres and climb the slab pretty much direct. The direct start is a shin-bruising 5c.

Left is a chimney and another steep buttress.

CR 16 **Long Climb** 15m HS *
The first and easily identifiable crack which leads to a chimney. Face left in this and exit via one of those horrible stomach traverses to the left before finishing up an easy break.

Left is a steep wall and then a chimney – Open Chimney D.

CR 17 **The Shelf** 13m E2 5c **
Start beneath the bulges at a groove right of the chimney. Up to a bulge and right to a pocket. Difficult moves will hopefully result in a standing position on the sloping shelf. Feels strenuous and precarious

The crag becomes split by ledges for a while now.

CR 18 **Sunstroke** 14m VS 4c *
The wall right of the V leads into the crack. The direct is good 5b. The next route takes the slim left to right trending gangway in a steepening slab just left of the last route.

CR(14–17), Crookrise Crag

CR (18–24)

CR 19 **Slip 'n' Slide** 8m E5 6b **
Increasingly desperate climbing and a tremendously impressive lead for its pre-Fire time.

CR 20 **Green Crack** 9m VS 4c

CR 21 **Knuckleduster** 9m VS 4c

CR 22 **Knuckle Crack** 9m VS 4c

Left again is a tall buttress and then a wide slab, set above a steeper wall and topped by a roof in its centre.

CR 23 **Walker's Farewell** 18m VS 4c *
A lower pitch up a left-slanting ramp is often neglected for the delightful upper slab. This is climbed centrally via a delicate mantel, then slightly left, still delicate, to a finish rightwards through a break.

CR 24 **Walkover** 12m E3 6a *
Start at the same point as the second part of the last climb. Very daintily along the bottom edge of the slab leftwards to a slightly easier finish up the arete.

Continuing left is a large blocky pinnacle, separated from the crag by Slingsby's Chimney VD.

CR 25 **Hovis** 12m E1 5c **
Start on a boulder at the front right-hand edge of the pinnacle. Step down off the boulder on to the face via some little pockets. A delightful sequence leads to an easing in the angle. Still delicate climbing leads up the arete on the right to the top.

CR(18–24), Crookrise Crag

Slingsby's chimney

Fly

CR (25–28)

CR 26 **Small Brown**   12m   E3   6a   *

The arete right of Slingsby's Chimney. Start by a rising traverse from the left or direct (harder). A route which still foils many budding rock athletes.

CR 27 **Crease**   13m   VS   4c

CR 28 **Crease Direct**

Takes the balancy groove direct at 5c. The impossible-looking wall just right is Fly 6b.

Rushlight 9m S is the good slab left of Crease. Well left of this area is some excellent bouldering including a splendid series of roof problems. There are also some excellent problems and routes on the boulders under the main face. The best routes are two VS's on the valley side of the large boulder. The Ruffian takes a brilliant line up a layback crack leading to the left edge of the boulder and The Urchin starts 6m right, mantels on to a ledge and follows a slim slab.

Deer Gallows   GR SD 995555

Situation and access

The crags lie in relatively grand isolation, high on the grouse moor about 15 minutes' walk east of Crookrise. Parking is as for Crookrise but, after leaving the road, strike up to the crag via a streamside path (about 15 minutes).

Character

Though the outcrop is small, both the rock and the routes tend to be good. The main wall faces south, but other routes face all points of the compass. In good weather the crag has a delightful ambience which, coupled with a lack of intensity, tights and crowds, makes a visit well worth while.

CR(25–28), Crookrise Crag

DG (1–8)

The climbs

Main Wall

This is the long wall which lies to the rear of the big block.

DG 1 **Rift Arete** 11m HVS 5b

DG 2 **The Pocket** 11m HVS 5b

DG 3 **Fist Crack** 11m VS 4c *
The satisfying jam crack and the steep flake above.

DG 4 **Balance** 13m VS 5a
Hard starting moves, then past a pocket to a ledge. Up the
corner and move right to a pleasant finish up the wall.

DG 5 **The Nose** 13m VS 4c

DG 6 **Cave Crack** 13m VS 5a **
Interesting crack climbing requiring varied technique.

DG 7 **Hangman's Wall** 12m HVS 5b

DG 8 **Deer Gallows Chimney** 12m D *

DG 9 **Deer Gallows Wall** 12m HVS 5a

DG 10 **Staircase Rib** 12m D
The left rib of the opposite wall.

DG 11 **The Cringe** 14m HVS 5b *
The slender crack that splits the roof of the cave is a tough
proposition and is reached by easier and wider cracks.

DG(1–8), Deer Gallows

DG (10–13)

DG 12 **Pinnacle Wall**   12m   S

DG 13 **Layman's Arete**   11m   D   **
  The wide crack and arete above give a pleasant and varied
  beginner's route.

Earl Crag   GR SD 988429

Situation and access
Earl Crag is easily seen on the skyline of the moor above and south-
east of the village of Cowling on the main Colne to Keighley road.
Two monuments on the moor top provide unmistakable landmarks.
The crag faces north-west and is approached via a small road from
the village of Cowling which runs over the moor to Oakworth.
Limited parking exists near the top of the hill and the rocks can then
be approached via a path which runs past a small quarry. Please
avoid approaching the crag directly and damaging walls.

Character
Probably the best time to visit the crag is on a sunny summer's
evening, when it makes an excellent venue. In windy weather and in
winter, conditions can be less pleasant due to the exposed nature of
the place. The rock is generally excellent grit and the crag is
composed of a number of separate buttresses which can be
approached by paths either under or on top of the crag.

The climbs
The routes are described from left to right. The first buttresses are
reached a couple of minutes past the small quarry. A good
identifying feature is the beautiful left to right slanting gangway of:

DG(10–13), Deer Gallows

EL (1–6)

EL 1 **Early Riser**   10m   E5   6a   ***
Attain a standing position on the gangway and follow it
precariously. A tiny hole on the left wall usually provides a
painfully crucial hold. Thin, serious and brilliant.

The next buttress has an undercut base on its left-hand side.

EL 2 **The Kipper**   16m   E3   5c   *
Climb the right side of the undercut area strenuously to the
large ledge. Finish up the right side of the arete above past a
hole near the top.

EL 3 **Erasor Slab**   8m   VS   5a   *
Start at the right side of the slab to the right of the last route.
Move up a little way to a toe traverse left. There are a few
ways of making the final moves to the ledge and none of
them feels easy.

EL 4 **Fishladder**   9m   HVS   5b   *
A good finish to the last route. The gangway round to the
left of the ledge is good but has an awkward start.

EL 5 **Problem Rib**   6m   VS   5a   *
Another finishing pitch. This one is the fine arctc on the
right of the ledge. An interesting move at half-height is the
crux.

EL 6 **Grey Wall**   7m   S

EL 7 **Mantelshelf Slab**   6m   S
Around 20m right is a slab containing some sizeable pockets.
Wander pleasantly up this.

EL(1–6), Earl Crag

EL (7-11)

EL(7–11), Earl Crag (left)

EL, Earl Crag, Erasor Slab
(right)

EL 8 **Pedestal Rib** 8m VS 4c **

A few metres right is a rib with a pedestal beneath its left
side. This splendid little route goes up from the pinnacle top
on pockets before moving right around the rib to finish.

EL 9 **Cave Traverse** 10m VS 4c

Right of this buttress and across a gully is a prominent
overhanging prow – the Indicator.

EL 10 **Flake Crack** 9m VS 4c *

The meaty jamming crack on the left of the Indicator. Feels
good.

EL 11 **Indicator Crack** 10m S

100 metres or so to the right is a wall. The next routes are on
a buttress just right of the wall.

EL(12–16), Earl Crag

EL 12 Green Rib 9m E1 5c

The rib on the left of the dirty corner crack has a technical and gymnastic lower section.

EL 13 Butterfly Crack VS 4c

EL 14 Shothole Ridge 9m VS 4c

Make a hard move on to a short slab right of the right-hand rib. Move left on to the rib and finish direct. The wall right of this is:

EL 15 Mantel Maniac

Gain the horizontal break and either traverse off right at 6a or make a manic mantel direct at E3 6b.

EL 16 Little Demon 7m VD

Main Buttress Area

This is the biggest buttress here and it has routes to match its size.

EL 17 **Desert Island Arete** 20m E5 6b ***
The first break on the left arete of the buttress is gained with great difficulty. After the next break, ascend the wall just right of the arete.

EL 18 **Viscount's Route** 17m HVS 5a *
The hanging crack on the front of the buttress is reached by a steady hand traverse from the right. Up the strenuous crack to a ledge. Finish up the corner crack.

EL(17–24), Earl Crag

EL (17–24)

Tiger traverses

EL (25–27)

25

26

27

EL 19 **Perch Wall** 19m HVS 5a **
Start as for the last route but traverse right below the strenuous crack on to the arete. Exposed and interesting climbing leads to the ledge and an easy finish. Good.

EL 20 **Earl Crack** 17m VS 4c **
The classic-looking corner crack to the right does not disappoint.

The wall left of the crack, but starting up it, is Liz's Wall E2 6a.

EL 21 **Earl Buttress** 16m E2 5c *
A good route up the centre of the wall right of Earl Crack.

EL 22 **Evasion** 11m E1 5b

EL 23 **Trite Rib** 11m E3 5c

EL 24 **Chockstone Crack** 7m S

Further right is the unmistakable Prow Buttress.

EL 25 **Tiger Wall** 14m HS **
Start up some slabs and reach a traverse line. Follow this with interest out to a fine position on the arete. Finish straight up on jugs.

The right wall of the Prow has two traverse lines – Tiger Traverses; the upper is VS and the lower HVS. Right of the Prow is an easy chimney. To the right of this is an attractive short slab.

EL(25–27), Earl Crag

EL 26 **Mousehole Slab** 8m   VS   4c   *

From the foot of the chimney, move right on to a slim ledge and scurry straight up past the mousehole.

EL 27 **Rat Juggling** 8m   VS   4c

Get on to the aforementioned ledge from the right and climb the blunt rib on sadly improved holds. There are some other excellent problems in this area including the sharp arete at 5c.

Eastby Crag   GR SE 023549

Situation and access

The crag is a short drive north-east of the village of Eastby. Park by a gate below the crag and before the obvious bends in the road. Approach the crag from here.

Character

Rough, pebbly gritstone, a fine south-facing situation and some first-class routes make this crag well worth a visit.

The climbs

These are described from left to right. The left of the crag is dominated by a tall, isolated buttress. The first route starts at the foot of this.

EB 1 **Pillar Front** 22m   E1   5a   ***

Vintage grit – serious and sustained. Climb a short rib to a small overhang. Over this and up to the left via a faint and thought-provoking ramp to a foothold on the left arete. Rock up right on to a small ledge and go boldly through the bulge, moving first right and then left up the final slab.

EL, Earl Crag, Tiger Wall

EB (1–8)

EB 2 **Pillar Rib**   18m   VS   4c   *

EB 3 **Eastby Buttress**   18m   VD   *

Climbs a variety of cracks on the right of the buttress. Good
holds and protection. A pleasant introduction to jamming.

EB 4 **The Padder**   18m   E1   5b   *

Climb the first section of Eastby Buttress until it is possible
to traverse right immediately above the roof on small
footholds to the centre of the slab. Balance up on pebbles
and friction. A good route, marred only by the half-way
ledge.

EB 5 **Whaup Edge**   18m   VS   4c   *

Ascends the right edge of the slab taken by The Padder.
Start right of the rib and move left on to it immediately
above the overhang. Elegant moves lead up the arete to the
upper slab which is slightly easier. Airy and interesting.

EB 6 **Swastika**   35m   HVS   5a   **

A traverse starting up easy rocks left of Pillar Front, gaining
a traverse line on that route above the bulge before moving
round the arete and continuing on to Whaup Edge and
finishing up this.

EB 7 **Crossing the Line**   15m   E2   5b

EB 8 **Broken Arete**   32m   M

A good beginner's route, unusually long for the area. Start
15m right of the previous route and follow the rock suggested
by the route name.

EB(1–8), Eastby Crag

EB (9–15)

EB 9 **Knuckle Slab**   13m   VS   4c
Starts at the foot of a slab 15m right of the previous route
which is topped by a split block. From the right-hand side,
tiptoe left and ascend the arete, from the top of which a
variety of finishes are available. The Index Variation is
equally good and follows a direct line up the slab via a
shallow scoop. Balancy.

EB 10 **Birch Tree Crack**   27m   HD

The next routes are on Nose Buttress, the first buttress met
when continuing right.

EB 11 **Nose Climb**   14m   S
Start on the left of the buttress at a horizontal crack.
Traverse this with a couple of nice surprises *en route* to the
nose. Pick a way up the slab to a short crack with bombproof
jams.

EB 12 **Thumper**   13m   E2   5b
Start at the same point as the last route. Climb a short
pocketed wall and pass a small roof on its left. A serious
route which packs a punch.

25m right is an easy angled slab topped by a roof with a
further green slab above it.

EB 13 **Mist Slab**   20m   VS   4b
Takes the lower slab, turning the roof on its left and
sneaking back right before sliding upwards again, whilst a
direct variation, HVS 5a, climbs the roof direct.

EB(9–15), Eastby Crag

EB 14 **Block Buttress** 8m VS 4c

      The next buttress is square cut and undercut at its foot. This route attacks the right-hand arete, using a thin crack to gain access to better holds, a rest and an easier finish.

EB 15 **Hangs** 8m E3 6a

      This route moves left from the resting place on the last route and climbs the centre of the buttress. The direct start is 6c and looks it.

Heptonstall Quarry GR SD 985277

Situation and access

Despite its proximity to civilization, the quarry is in a rather elevated position on the edge of Heptonstall village, which is just outside Hebden Bridge. The church provides a useful landmark for the approach. Park near some old garages behind it, or on the road just before them. (Building work here may affect parking at the old garages in the future.) A well-marked path leads down from the end of the garages between two walls to an open area where the crag lies directly below. Descend via some steps on the right when facing out.

Character

This sizeable crag has some first-class climbing on a generally hard and fine-grained sandstone. It faces south-west, dries quickly and provides some exposed and high-quality climbs which are longer than those on most of the comparable crags in the area.

The climbs

After descending the steps, an attractive and sizeable wall can be seen on the left. Directly opposite it is a large boulder of good-quality grit, whose quarry-facing side has some excellent bouldering.

                                      HQ, Heptonstall Quarry, Fairy Steps

HQ (1–9)

The first routes lie on a wall on the left of the quarry which meets it at an angle. They are described from left to right.

HQ 1 **Curving Crack** 15m VS 4c **
    The striking curving jamming crack gives good value.

HQ 2 **Main Line** VS 16m 4c
    A pleasant line up the wall just right of the crack.

The Red Wall

This is the first major wall of the quarry.

HQ 3 **Thin Red Line** 20m E1 5b ***
    The first weakness on the wall to a break. Go right and up a crack to the finish of Pulpit Route. Highly recommended.

HQ 4 **Hard Line** 20m E5 6b *

HQ 5 **Demerara** 21m E3 6a *

HQ 6 **Brown Sugar** 20m E2 5c **
    Climb the cracks behind the tree, with an excursion right then back left at 6 metres. A well protected and enjoyable climb.

HQ 7 **Pulpit Route** 26m VS 4c *
    Ascend a series of ledges leftwards from the right end of Red Wall. An obvious traverse left leads to some cracks and a chimney exit. A direct start is possible at 5c, up a right-slanting line of holds starting 3m left of the original route.

HQ 8 **A Step in the Green Light** 25m E6 6b **
    A serious direct line.

HQ(1–9), Heptonstall Quarry

HQ 9 Cream   26m   E4   6a   *
The scary arete just right.

Yellow Wall

The steep wall set slightly back and split in its centre by a
magnificent crack.

HQ 10 Trepidation   22m   VS   4c   **
The enticing corner is quitted after 10m for cracks in the left
wall. Mantel on to a ledge and continue direct.

HQ 11 Fairy Steps Direct   22m   VS   4c   *
The corner direct to the ledge. Exit round to the left from
here and up ledges.

HQ 12 Fairy Steps   25m   S   ***
An atmospheric route taking steep ground at an easy
standard. The wall right of the corner leads to a cave, from
which a rising ascent leftwards gains the good ledge. Belay
possible. Continue round to the left to an easy but exposed
finish.

HQ 13 Forked Lightning Crack   23m   E2   5c   ***
The most striking line in the quarry. Big friends protect the
route well, but don't make it feel any easier.

HQ 14 Bull's Crack   25m   VS   4c   ***
A classic and popular route giving varied crack climbing.
1. 16m 4c. The corner leads past a bulging section to a belay
on the Rabbit Ledge.
2. 9m. The awkward chimney on the left.

HQ(10–18), Heptonstall Quarry

HQ 15 **Senility**   13m   HVS   5a   *

The wall right of the corner leads to a hop out on to the Rabbit Ledge.

HQ 16 **Grindley's Grunt/Monkey Puzzle**   29m   HVS   5a   4c

1. 16m 5a. The break in the roof on to the Rabbit Ledge.
2. 13m 4c. Up the wall towards its left-hand side. Traverse right and finish more or less direct.

Lower Quarry

This section has generally poorer rock, but the following routes are well worth while.

HQ 17 **Sunstroke Slab**   19m   HS   **

1. 12m. Climb to below the eye-catching corner crack and traverse the slab to the right into a corner.
2. 7m. The groove.

HQ 18 **Triplex Direct**   34m   HVS   5a   5a   **

Start at the left side of the lower section of the quarry.
1. 21m 5a. Climb the wall and traverse left under the roof. Eventually gain a slab which leads to a belay under the curving corner.
2. 13m 5a. The handsome curving corner.

HQ, Heptonstall Quarry, Senility

IK (1-3)

Ilkley Crags   GR SE 130467

Situation and access
There are two main climbing areas here, the Cow and Calf section
which includes the quarry and is easily visible from the road, and
Rocky Valley which lies just over half a mile away on the moor.
From Ilkley, take the road signed 'Cow and Calf' and follow this to
a parking area on the right just before the Cow and Calf Hotel. The
Cow and Calf group, including the quarry, can be seen from here
and is easily reached in a couple of minutes. To get to Rocky Valley,
either scramble out of the back of the quarry or skirt it on its left and
aim for the conspicuous crags half a mile or so away. All the crags
are rather exposed, Rocky Valley especially so, and most sections
face north and east. Rather than providing shelter, the quarry often
seems to act as a wind tunnel.

Character
Apart from being an excellent climbing area, the Cow and Calf
group is a popular tourist attraction and dog-walking location, so be
prepared for audiences, noise and litter. Although the rock in the
quarry is not as rough as the natural grit here, it makes up for this
with some fine cracks and a tendency towards square-cut holds. The
rock on The Cow and The Calf is first-class gritstone. Rocky Valley
is a real contrast, being an altogether quieter place. The rock is good
and some of the buttresses have more of a mountain feel about them.

The climbs
These are described in four separate groups.
    From the car-park, the quarry entrance can be seen clearly, and
to the right the large natural edge – The Cow – and the huge
boulder in front of it:

   The Calf (the boulder everyone wants in their back garden)

IK(1–3), Ilkley, The Calf

IK (4–16)

The severely overhanging wall facing the road has three hard routes.

IK 1 **Gnome**   E1   5c
The strenuous fault line on the right requires an athletic approach. The centre of the wall, with a left trending finish, is 6c and the apparently holdless thin crack to the left is 7a.

Round to the right is a slab.

IK 2 **Pebble Groove**   HVS   5b
The slim, slanting groove up the left of the slab is delicate. (The foot of the slab has been sadly defaced with a paint which considerably reduces the friction available.)

IK 3 **Late Fever**   E5   6c
A desperate-looking line up the right-hand side of the slab.

The Cow

The first two routes are on a buttress about 150m right of The Cow.

IK 4 **Patlence**   8m   VS   4c   *
A bonny little route which climbs a short left-facing ramp and a short wall.

IK 5 **Lost Boots**   8m   VS   4c

IK 6 **Hand Jive**   15m   HVS   5b

IK 7 **Milky Way**   18m   E5   6b   ***
On the right side of The Cow is an all too obvious peg-scarred crack, which is hard all the way.

IK(4–16), Ilkley, The Cow

IK 8 **Galaxy** 18m E6 6b **

The scoop right of Milky Way, gained from that route.

IK 9 **New Statesman** 17m E8 6c ***

The incredible right arete of The Cow. An amazing solution to a long-standing problem.

IK 10 **Mad Dogs** 17m E4 6a

IK 11 **Cow Udder** 10m HVS 5a

A sadly chipped but interesting route reminiscent of a climbing wall.

IK 12 **Desperate Dan** 11m E6 6b **

The left arete of The Cow with a hard and committing start. The rest of it isn't exactly a picnic.

IK 13 **'A' Climb** 31m VD ***

A climb of real character and not easy for its grade.
1. 10m. The chimney left of the arete leads to a cave.
2. 12m. Hunch rightwards to a crack, climb this on surprising holds to another rightwards traverse via a huge flake to an exposed stance.
3. 9m. Follow the line above to a smooth and fitting finale. A good variation finish is Ferdinand 12m S, which traverses right from the second stance and finishes via a couple of short slabs.

IK 14 **Cow Rib** 7m VS 4c *

Exposed and delicate.

IK 15 **Chiseller** 11m S

IK 16 **Ladybird** 11m VD

IK, Ilkley, Short Circuit

IK (17–31)

The Quarry

IK 17 **Flake Crack** 9m   S

Ik 18 **Botterill's Crack** 14m   VS   4c

IK 19 **Walewska** 14m   VS   4c   **
Takes a prominent curving line in the upper part of the wall,
reached via a short corner. A satisfying route.

IK 20 **Waterloo** 14m   E3   6a

IK 21 **Josephine** 14m   HS   *
The polished break in this wall leads to a ledge system and
possible belay. Continue left to a niche and a short groove to
finish.

IK 22 **Tufted Crack** 7m   E2   5c   *
The short, gradually flaring crack in the upper wall can be
frustrating in its centre. Well naughty.

IK 23 **Blucher** 14m   VS   4c

IK 24 **Napoleon** 14m   VS   4c   *
The first pitch of Josephine again, followed by a steep crack
with good finishing jams.

IK 25 **Hipgnosis** 14m   E4   6b

IK 26 **Short Circuit** 9m   E1   5c   *
A difficult move on chips leads to a neat mantel on to a slim
ledge. Up the arete on the left and mantel to easier ground
and a variety of exits.

IK(17–31), Ilkley, The Quarry

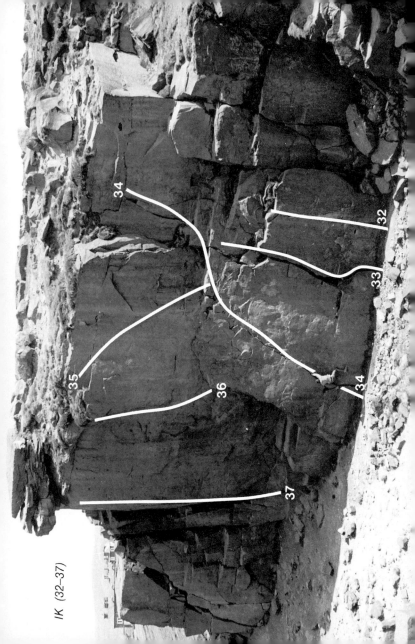

IK (32–37)

IK 27 **Little John**   9m   HVS   5b

IK 28 **Josephine Direct**   14m   S   *
Twin cracks lead to an avoidance strategy right and up
before returning left to finish. The Direct is slightly harder.

IK 29 **Fairy Steps**   14m   MS
A popular route, both in ascent and descent, up the slab left
of the chimney.

IK 30 **'S' Crack**   14m   VS   4c   **
Good climbing up the S-shaped cracks with good holds
materializing on demand. The wall to the right is Fairy Wall
HVS 5a.

IK 31 **Old Crack**   14m   VS   4b
The next crack to the left with a wider upper section.

A rockfall left of here casts some doubt as to the stability of
the whole quarry! The fine arete at the back of the quarry is
Guillotine E5 6a. The arete is tackled on its left until a
switch right is made at the chipped hold. The left side of the
quarry has some good short routes.

IK 32 **Peg Crack**   6m   HVS   5a

IK 33 **Letter Box Crack**   8m   S

IK 34 **Curving Cracks**   17m   VS   5a
The cracks are just a little slim for comfortable jamming, but
holds on the right help. From the ledge (a few friable holds)
some more cracks on the right lead to the top.

IK 35 **High Street**   8m   E1   5b

IK(32–37), Ilkley, The Quarry

IK (37–44)

IK 36 **Snap Decision**   15m   E7   6c
:   High numbers and horrendous-looking climbing up the
    hanging groove to the left of the last route. A couple of pegs
    mark the way – your lead.

IK 37 **Wellington Crack**   15m   E4   5c   ***
:   The superb peg-scarred crack.

    Left of here are a number of poorer routes. Wellington
    Chimney D is the right-hand chimney, and the wall furthest
    left and right-slanting chimney are Nailbite VD.
        Left of the quarry entrance is a buttress split by some thin
    cracks.

IK 38 **Stickyfingers**   14m   E2   5b

IK 39 **Transparent Wall**   13m   HVS   5a   *
:   Climb the left-hand of two peg-scarred cracks to moves up
    and left to a ledge and welcome rest. A slender crack and an
    easier slab to finish.

IK 40 **Piton Wall**   13m   VS   5a   *
:   A delicate climb again up a tiny ramp which eventually
    leads to a small ledge. Past a pocket to an easy finish. Top
    end.

IK 41 **Serendipity**   11m   E2   5c

    Another, larger-looking buttress to the left provides the next
    routes.

IK 42 **Doris's Route**   17m   VD
:   From the left edge of the buttress, gain the slab via chipped
    holds, traverse to its centre and climb direct.

IK(37–44), Ilkley, Piton Wall area

RV (1-9)

IK 43 **Blackball**   14m   E2   5c

IK 44 **Bald Pate**   18m   VS   5a

Rocky Valley   GR SE 122464

The buttresses and climbs are all described from left to right.

Number One Buttress

RV 1 **Cooper's Slab**   8m   D
The slab above the fallen block is gained from the left.

RV 2 **Beeline**   12m   HVS   5a   ***
The brilliant jamming crack is reached via the undercut wall
with a hard move to get into the first good jams.

RV 3 **Beyond the Fringe**   12m   E4   6a   **
A continuously technical route which can be protected from
Beeline if desired. Start below faint grooves right of Beeline
and make a very difficult move to a good jug. Continue up
the next vague line which is slightly less difficult but still
sustained.

RV 4 **Little 'A' Climb**   9m   S

Number Two Buttress

RV 5 **Stiction**   8m   VS

RV 6 **Stiction Chimney**   8m   D

RV 7 **Scoop and Hole**   8m   VS   4c   *

RV(1–9), Rocky Valley, Buttresses One and Two

RV (10–22)

RV 8 **The Strid** 9m S

RV 9 **Flypaper** 5m S
A glossy problem left of the pod, which itself provides an amusing problem.

Number Three Buttress

This is easily recognized by a slab split by three horizontal cracks.

RV 10 **Three Slabs Route** 9m MS

RV 11 **The Flake Climb** 16m S **
Gain the flake from the right and surmount it in an excellent position.

RV 12 **Bogey Wall/Hades** 14m VS 4c
A polished wall leads to a direct ascent of the left edge of the next wall and, in turn, the flake of the last route.

RV 13 **Oak Tree Slab** 9m S
The green and chipped slab leads to a roof which is turned either way.

Number Four Buttress

An impressive buttress split by some striking lines.

RV 14 **Sentry Box** 9m S
Gain the niche by a crack and exit direct.

RV(10–22), Rocky Valley, Buttresses Three and Four

RV (23–27)

RV 15 **Kestrel**   11m   VS   4c   *
The testing off width to the right leads to the niche.

RV 16 **Shock Horror**   11m   E5   6a   **
Start as for the last route, but swing right on to the
unprotected rib where pockets lead upwards. Nasty landing.

RV 17 **Slide Zone**   8m   E4   6a
A blank groove and ensuing wall round to the right.

RV 18 **Twin Cracks**   8m   VS   4c

RV 19 **Somersault**   8m   VS   4c   **
The stout jamming crack.

RV 20 **Long Chimney**   13m   D

RV 21 **Sound Box**   12m   HS
No problem into the recess. Exit awkwardly and climb the
crack above the ledge.

RV 22 **Tomb Stone Crack**   13m   HS

Number Five Buttress

A smaller crag at a slightly higher level.

RV 23 **Blasphemy Crack**   8m   S
The evil crack on the left of the buttress.

RV 24 **The Chute**   9m   S
An awkward narrow slab which has lost some of its friction.

RV(23–27), Rocky Valley, Number Five Buttress

RV (28–44)

RV 25 Gym Crack 8m HVS 5a **
A delightful little jamming problem.

RV 26 Sylvia 8m E1 5c
A difficult problem up the peg-scarred line right of Gym
Crack and finishing up flat holds in the wall above.

RV 27 Sylveste 10m HVS 5b *
An awkward mantel across to the right leads to a traverse
back left to the Sylvia finish.

Number Six Buttress

This is the largest in Rocky Valley and is a short walk
further to the right.

RV 28 Catapult Crack 8m VS 4c

RV 29 Sunburst Finish 8m E5 6a

RV 30 Gutsie 8m VS 4c

RV 31 Stump Chimney 8m VS 4c

RV 32 Blind Valley 11m E3 5c *
The old peg crack.

RV 33 Countdown to Disaster 13m E8 6c ***
The incredible arete has a potentially terminal fall factor.

RV 34 Brush Crack 12m S
Reach the corner crack and climb it pleasantly.

RV 35 Arrowhead 13m S

RV(28–44), Rocky Valley, Number Six Buttress

RV 36 **Windy Buttress** 9m VS 4c

A steep, short wall leads to a ledge. An inverted V-shaped crack leads to a cave and a finishing crack.

RV 37 **The Ogre** 12m VS 4c *

Reach the overhanging crack and climb it entertainingly.

RV 38 **Matchbox** 13m S

RV 39 **Overhanging Chockstone Crack** 7m D

RV 40 **Double Chockstone Crack** 8m S

RV 41 **Holly Tree Route** 16m D

RV 42 **Spreadeagle** 16m S **

From the right end of the crag, hand traverse left along a flake to a block. Get into a scoop on the left which leads to the top.

RV 43 **Bald Eagle** E2 5c

RV 44 **Illegitimate Crack** 14m VS 4c *

From the flake at the foot of Spreadeagle follow a series of cracks of different widths to the top.

Penyghent GR 836732

Situation and access

A high-level crag lying on the edge of the summit plateau of Penyghent. From Horton-in-Ribblesdale, follow the green lane towards Hull Pot and from the end of the enclosed lane aim directly for the crag from an appropriate point (approx. one hour); or from

PG, Penyghent, Christian's Crux

Dale Head, which is on the Stainforth to Halton Gill road, follow the Pennine Way to the top of the crags, an easier and shorter approach (half an hour).

Character
The highest and remotest crag in this section, with an atmosphere to match. The routes described are exposed and, although the rock is sometimes variable in quality, the situation and views make everything well worth the walk-in.

The climbs
These are described from left to right.

PG (1–7)

PG 1 **Agnostic's Arete** 16m S

PG 2 **Red Pencil Direct** 27m MS **
A popular route taking a good line on steep rock. Scramble
over broken rock to the foot of a big groove. This leads up to
the roof, from where a move right leads to a short finishing
wall. A steep and exciting climb. It is also possible to finish
left beneath the roof at VD standard, or to climb straight
through it via:

PG 3 **Gladiator** 27m VS 4c *
A direct finish through the overhangs above the groove of
Red Pencil.

PG 4 **Damocles Groove** 27m S **
A fine line right of Red Pencil.

PG 5 **Brass Monkey** 27m VS 4c

PG 6 **Christian's Crux** 25m VS 4c **
A pleasant short wall leads up to the roof. Move right and
continue up steep rock which is well supplied with jugs.

Across to the right is a short wall higher up split by a
striking crackline.

PG 7 **Pitchfork Crack** 23m HVS 5a **
Easy climbing to the foot of the beautiful jamming crack.

Other easy routes and scrambles with a mountaineering
flavour can be found further right.

PG(1–7), Penyghent

WP (1-3)

Widdop   GR SD 934324

Situation and access
The crag lies just above Widdop reservoir, which can be found on
the Burnley or Nelson to Hebden Bridge road. Parking is possible
near the dam wall, allowing easy access to the rocks.

Character
A high-level, north-facing crag which gets very green in wet
weather. Many holds on the older routes are well polished, but in
general the rock is the usual high-quality gritstone. Good routes of
all grades can be found here, along with some excellent bouldering,
in a wild Pennine setting which enhances the experience. The only
disappointing feature is the profusion of chipped holds.

The climbs
To the left of the biggest buttress is Cave Buttress. The climbs here,
as on the other buttresses, are described from left to right.

WP 1 **Curving Crack**   16m   VS   4c   *
       The attractive left-hand crack.

WP 2 **Cave Crack**   14m   VS   4c

WP 3 **Cave Arete**   12m   E2   5c

       The largest, central buttress is Mystery Buttress, which has
       some pleasant and quite long routes.

WP 4 **Ordinary Route**   31m   VD   **
       Start on the right of a large block at the foot of the crag.
       From the third ledge, grovel right to the Bull's Horns and so
       reach the fourth ledge, from where a traverse right again
       leads to a chimney and the top.

WP(1–3), Widdop, Cave Buttress

WP (4–9)

WP(4–9), Widdop, Mystery
Buttress (left)

WP, Widdop, Ordinary
Route (right)

WP 5 **The Three Cs**   27m   VS   4c

WP 6 **Krypton Route**   23m   S   **
After the groove, finish via the ordinary route, or better by:

WP 7 **The Flake**   HS
The left-hand line in the headwall; or

WP 8 **The Layback**   VS   4c
The right-hand crack in the headwall.

WP 9 **Wrinkled Wall**   14m   VD   *
The crack on the right of the wall right of the gully leads to a
small ledge. Finish direct.

WP (11–13)

WP 10 Wrinkled Wall Direct   13m   MVS   4b
A direct on the last route, climbing the wall direct to the small ledge and finishing up the groove on the right.

Across to the right is the Overhang Group.

WP 11 Ceiling Crack   E1   5b   ***
The left-hand line in the big roof is a classical Whillans product. Originally VS, it would probably give an ordinary VS leader nightmares.

WP 12 '30 Seconds over Winterland'   E4   6a   ***
An outstanding roof problem taking the right-hand crack. A difficult start leads to reasonable jamming out of the horizontal.

WP 13 Celebrity Buttress   11m   VS   4c
The crack in the small buttress to the right. Traversing in from the left is good but harder.

WP 14 Piton Crack   9m   HVS   5a   *
Takes the line of a heavily peg-scarred crack on a small crag just before the Purgatory Buttress.

WP 15 Eccentric Solution   9m   E3   6b

The large crag across to the right is Purgatory or Guinea Pig Buttress.

WP 16 Afternoon Delight   19m   E4   6a   *

WP 17 Swift and Sure   20m   E5   6b   **
A fine route with a rounded finish.

WP(11–13), Widdop, The Overhang area

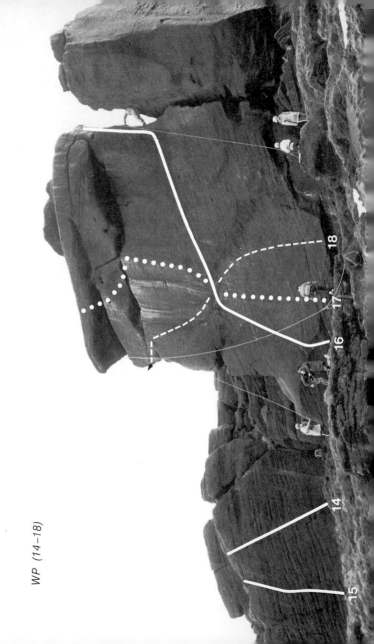

WP (14–18)

WP 18 The Artificial Route   VS   4c   **

A chipped start leads to an enjoyable traverse and a bold
finish.

Bouldering Areas

Bride Stones   GR SD 928269
A first-class bouldering area which is well worth an evening visit. It
can be found alongside the Hebden Bridge to Burnley road, 100m
on the Burnley side of the Sportsman's Inn, on the left.

Hugencroft   GR SD 924275
Another good bouldering area which has suffered from access
problems, so act with the usual courtesy. Approach as for the Bride
Stones and go a little further towards Burnley, where the rocks can
be seen on the right.

Hetchell Crag (Pompey Caley)   GR SE 376424
An excellent bouldering and training area which also has some very
hard, short routes. Worth a visit if you're in the area. Many of the
obvious lines are not too hard, but there are some difficult problems
on the main wall. The rock is not wonderful, being a soft gritstone,
but it is very climbable. The crag is in a nature reserve, Hetchell
Wood, and can be approached from the main Leeds to Wetherby
road. The nearest named place is Bardsey, and a bridleway/disused
railway line leads off the main road near Bank Top Garage. Follow

WP(14–18), Widdop, Purgatory Buttress

this to a halt at a missing bridge and the crag lies in the woods
across to the left.

Shipley Glen   GR SE 131389
An excellent and popular bouldering crag, with some of the
'problems' a little long for comfortable jump-offs. The rock is good-
quality grit which has once more suffered shamefully at the hands of
the phantom chippers. The Glen and the adjacent Countryside
Centre are signposted from Baildon, which is a couple of miles north
of Shipley, and cars can be parked close to the top of the crag.

Woodhouse Scar   GR SD 083235
An excellent bouldering crag on the outskirts of Halifax. Approach
via King's Cross and Skircoat Moor Road. The crags are adjacent to
the Albert Promenade. Though there are a number of routes here,
their individual description is unnecessary, and it is best treated as a
training area.

HC, Hetchell Crag

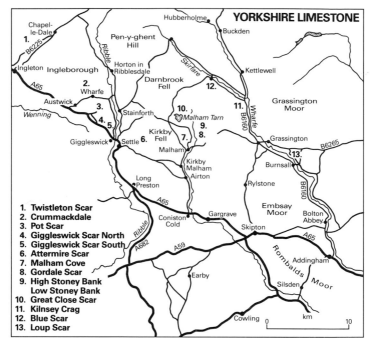

1. **Twistleton Scar**
2. **Crummackdale**
3. **Pot Scar**
4. **Giggleswick Scar North**
5. **Giggleswick Scar South**
6. **Attermire Scar**
7. **Malham Cove**
8. **Gordale Scar**
9. **High Stoney Bank**
   Low Stoney Bank
10. **Great Close Scar**
11. **Kilnsey Crag**
12. **Blue Scar**
13. **Loup Scar**

Yorkshire Limestone

Limestone

Attermire Scar   GR SD 834642 (and surrounding area)

Situation and access
The Scar is actually a series of crags which generally face south-
west. The best approach is to follow the Kirby Malham road from
Settle for about a mile and a half to a parking area on the left just
past a lane which leads to Stockdale Farm. Go up the lane and over
a stile on the left. The path leads over a gentle incline to reveal a
'wild west' scene, characterized by a rounded 'pap'. The Main
Buttress and its associated crags lie to the left, whilst Barrel Buttress
is easily seen lower down and to the right. The Escarpment is the
long section of crag a few hundred yards to the right. Please take
care not to damage walls whilst approaching any of the crags.

Character
Though the crags catch plenty of sunshine, they are also exposed to
the prevailing winds and can be quite bleak at times. The rock is
mostly good, but it is not as juggy as that of some of the other crags
in the area. The pitches here are generally quite short, but they
often pack a lot of climbing into their length and can feel much
bigger than they are. The unique appearance of the area and its
apparent isolation make it a very pleasant place to climb.

The climbs

The Main Buttress

This crag is composed of two tiers and is identified by the
large overhang in the middle of the lower tier.

Lower Tier
The routes are described from right to left.

AT 1 **Recessed Slab** 14m   HVS   5b   **
Originally graded VS in anger by Allan Austin after Tony
Greenbank snatched the first ascent with a fine lead. About
7m left of a small cave at the right of the lower tier is a dark
slab above a short steep wall. Climb the wall right of the slab
via a jug to a pocket, from where a 'playing the piano' move
leads left on to the slab. Continue without much respite up
the corner to the ledge. The direct start is 6a. A few metres
left is a hanging flake crack.

AT 2 **Amber Gambler** 26m   E3   6a   ***
1. 14m 6a. Reach the hanging flake awkwardly, think green
light and follow it to some vegetation and the ledge.
2. 12m 6a. Climb the wall just left of the belay, trend right
to a thin crack and storm up the final steep wall. A first-class
route.

AT 3 **Technically Speeding** 14m   E4   6b

AT 4 **Main Overhang** 12m   E3   6b
The crack splitting the big roof and the flake above. Well
protected, but not a wimp's route.

AT 5 **Ex-friend** 12m   E5   6c

AT 6 **Comer** 13m   E2   5b   *
The corner at the left end of the roofs, moving left at the top.

AT, Attermire Scar, Recessed Slab

AT (1–18)

Upper tier

Lower tier

AT 7 **Brutus** 13m E2 5c **

    The cracks left of Comer give an excellent, forearm-taxing route. The hanging crack high on the left of the Brutus wall and gained via undercuts from a short way up that route is Blind Panic, a sound E4 6a.

AT 8 **Blind Panic** 13m E4 6a *

AT 9 **Matador** 13m VS 4c *

    The first obvious groove to the left provides a pleasant outing with a gymnastic move a short way up providing the crux.

AT 10 **Mellow Yellow** 14m HVS 5a *

    The next groove, shallower and a little harder than Matador. It is normal to make a move left at the top of the groove.

AT 11 **Unchained** 14m VS 4c

    The undercut corner to the left.

AT 12 **Census** 10m HS

    The short wall and slab left again.

Upper Tier

These routes can be used as second pitches to Lower Tier routes. They are described from left to right.

AT 13 **Layback** 11m S

    A detached block on the terrace is a good landmark. This climb ascends the steep corner 6m left of the block, before moving left to a crack on the front of the buttress.

AT 14 **Stiction** 11m S

    The curving crack in the left wall of the recess.

AT(1–18), Attermire Scar, Main Buttress

AT (19–24)

AT 15 **Broken Chimney** VD

AT 16 **Determination** 12m HS 4b
The corner containing an elderberry tree.

AT 17 **Layby** 11m HS 4b *
The next striking corner crack provides a classic little route
which can prove to be a struggle.

The unfinished crack on the left-hand wall is TDC E2 6a.

AT 18 **Tipster** 11m E2 5c **
A thin crack right of Layby is climbed to a direct finish over
the roof.

Apex Buttress

Round to the left of the Main Buttress is Apex Buttress,
which is split into three tiers.

First Tier
The climbs are described from left to right. This tier consists
of a short wall about 50m long, which makes up for a lack of
stature with a daunting steepness.

AT 19 **Lugubrious** 8m E2 5b *
At the left-hand end of this section is a large double
overhang. This route ascends the undercut crack on the right
of this section. To the right is a smooth wall and a left-facing
corner.

AT 20 **Pythagoras** 8m S **
The excellent little corner.

AT(19–24), Attermire Scar, Apex Buttress, First Tier

AT (25–26)

AT 21 Flight of the Condor   8m   E3   5c   *
The middle of the wall right of Pythagoras gives a sustained route that has its moments.

Right are Twin Grooves, HVS 5b and right again an overhanging wall.

AT 22 Banana Crack   8m   E2   6a
The left-hand overhanging crack gives an intense struggle.

AT 23 Overhanging Crack   8m   HVS   5a
The awkward right-hand crack is easier but still a struggle.

AT 24 Trudge   8m   VS   4c   (Traditional)   **
This frustrating problem takes the next groove to the right, with the crux at the bottom. Actually, it might just warrant HVS 5b.

The crag now forms a bay and then opens out again into an attractive short wall, which is on the corner between the last routes and the Main Buttress.

AT 25 Richard the Turd   8m   E2   5c   *
A fine series of moves leads to the ledge, which is not quite as accommodating as it appears. Ascend the crack above.

AT 26 Halcyon Days   9m   E1   5b
As for Richard to the ledge, but climb the fault at the right end of the ledge.

Right is a crack which ends just too high from the ground. A monster dyno at E3 6b or combined tactics could bring success on White Lies.

AT(25–26), Attermire Scar, Apex Buttress, First Tier

Second Tier
The climbs are described from right to left.

AT 27 **Topsy Turvy** 7m   VD
A wall streaked with vertical cracks at the right-hand end of
the crag.

AT 28 **Smitton by Anguish** 8m   E1   5c
Left of an obvious easy corner (Purgatory 8m D) is a good-
looking wall. This route climbs painfully up a crozzly wall to
a slot, a break and a steep finish.

AT 29 **Jaws** 9m   HVS   5b   *
Another ex-VS! This one ascends the next crack to the left.

AT 30 **Alcove Slab** 9m   VD   *
The wall round the corner to the left and at right angles to
the Jaws wall. A happy little route which can be improved
by moving on to the right arete near the top.

Third Tier
Less continuous than the lower tiers, but with good
bouldering and some fine short routes, which are described
from right to left. Two smooth walls provide landmarks.

AT 31 **'A' Climb** 9m   MS
Locate an A-shaped crack in the upper part of a wall some
way to the right of the right-hand smooth wall. Gain it and
climb it.

AT 32 **Thank God** 9m   HVS   5b
The right-hand smooth wall. Aim for twin cracks in the
upper section via a tricky wall.

AT(31–33), Attermire Scar, Apex Buttress, Third Tier

AT (34-39)

AT 33 **Newsreader's Delight**   9m   HVS   5a
A slim crack on the right side of the left-hand smooth wall
provides the start. Scratch up the crack and continue up the
wall above.

Legover Groove Area

This can be located by walking left from the First Tier of
Apex Buttress past a grassy break. 10m left of the right-hand
end of the crag is a crack/groove curving left to right at first,
and finishing in a thin gully. This is:

AT 34 **Legover Groove**   16m   HVS   5b

AT 35 **Graphite Groove**   17m   HVS   5b   *
3m right of Legover Groove is a wall leading to a loose
section under the overhang. Climb a little corner on the right
and move left to a ledge and easier ground.

Left of Legover Groove is a right-facing corner crack:

AT 36 **Lantern Crack**   15m   HVS   5a

AT 37 **Red Light**   20m   HVS   5b   ***
A fingery start leads to lovely climbing up the crozzly wall
and a rising traverse to the right under the overhangs.

AT 38 **Blue Light**   15m   E1   6b
Start at the right end of a slabby wall. A mesmeric problem
start gives way to easier ground. Tough, and getting tougher.

AT 39 **Ginger**   15m   S   *
Weaves a juggy way up the left-hand side of the slabby wall.
A couple of metres left of here is a thin crack starting 3m up.

AT(34–39), Attermire Scar, Red Light area

AT (40—44)

This is Neon Crack E1 5c. The short hanging corner right of the cave is Hank S and the rough wall 2m right is Legal Limit E3 6a.

South-west Buttress

This can be located by continuing to walk left from the last area. The routes are described from right to left. At the right end of the crag is a deep and unmistakable corner groove.

AT 40 **Black Groove**   14m   VD   *
The aforementioned right-facing corner.

AT 41 **Wrinkle Slab**   10m   VD   *
Start a few metres left of the corner under the right-hand of two overhangs. Follow a groove in the wrinkly slab and make a move right when the rock steepens.

AT 42 **Slanting Slab**   12m   HS   *
A left-trending slab beneath the left-hand roof, moving right to finish.

The next routes are located from a 1m high flake under an attractive wall.

AT 43 **Overlapping Wall**   15m   HVS   5a   *
A direct line up to and over the overlap a couple of metres right of the flake.

AT 44 **Flower Power**   15m   MVS   4b   *
Start at the 1m flake. Make a move up and stretch left for a pleasant surprise. Go up a little corner and finish up the wall above.

AT(40–44), Attermire Scar, South-west Buttress

AT (45–50)

Barrel Buttress

This area can be found across to the right from the Main Buttress and at a lower level. Pinnacle Face looks towards the Main Buttress and Barrel Face can be found round the corner facing south.

Pinnacle Face
The climbs are described from left to right.

AT 45 **Straight Crack**   6m   VD

AT 46 **Spider Wall**   6m   HS   4b   *
A gymnastic little route with a puzzling mantel to finish. Excellent.

AT 47 **Spider's Web**   7m   E1   5b
The wall just to the right is equally good.

The gully has a flake crack on its right.

AT 48 **Flakey**   10m   S
A worthwhile route up the flake and wall.

AT 49 **Time Machine**   17m   HS   *
Start half-way between the last route and the pinnacle. Aim for twin cracks via a bulge a few metres up. From the ledge at the end of the cracks, move left to finish up similar ground to Flakey.

AT 50 **Fantasy**   20m   MS   *
1. 6m. The polished south-west rib of the pinnacle requires thought.
2. 14m. On to the main face and ascend on good holds for a

AT(45–50), Attermire Scar, Barrel Buttress

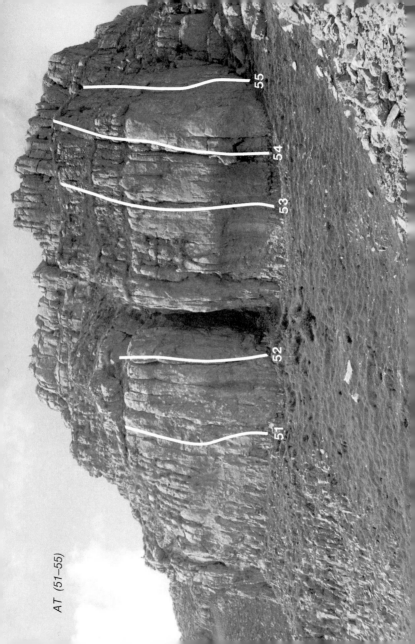

AT (51-55)

few metres before gaining a slanting fault on the left and a ledge. Move left again and climb a short wall.

Right of the pinnacle is a series of corners, and round further is:

Barrel Face
The routes are described from left to right. A gully splits the face. The first climb is 3m to the left.

AT 51 **Viper Direct**   12m   E1   5b
A narrow crack and wall above, left of the chimney crack.

AT 52 **Quad Crack**   12m   E1   5b   ***
The blatant crack just left of the gully is increasingly swinish, and feels at the top end of its grade.

AT 53 **Flagon Crack**   12m   HVS   5b   **
The first hard-looking crack right of the gully. A classy little pitch which is surprisingly sustained.

AT 54 **Plumbline**   12m   HVS   5b   *
A brutal pull sometimes gains the crack over the bulge which then eases.

AT 55 **Cooper's Wall**   VS   5a   *
A direct line up the centre of the glossy wall round the corner to the right. Don't be put off by the state of the first footholds!

The Escarpment

A few hundred metres up from and across to the right from Barrel Buttress is a long escarpment. The best routes are on

AT(51–55), Attermire Scar, Barrel Buttress

AT (56–58)

56

57

58

the right-hand end, where the crag is at its highest. The routes are described from right to left. At the extreme right of the escarpment is a cave – Horseshoe Cave.

AT 56 **Moonshine**   25m   HS   **

Left of the cave is an excellent wall. This route ascends the crack on its right-hand side, with a groove to finish.

AT 57 **Hare's Wall**   22m   VS   4c   **

Start below the overhang. Gain a small ledge and continue gingerly up the flakes to a bolt under the roof. Avoid the main part of the roof by climbing a steep crack on the left, but then traverse back right above the roof to a groove and cracks which lead to the top. The name of the route arises from the tortoise-like speed of the first ascensionists.

AT 58 **Direct Start/Hare Grip**   22m   HVS   5b   *

Start a couple of metres left of Hare's Wall at a dark wall. Reach the left-hand side of the roof, traverse right and pull through the roof via a groove on the right.

Blue Scar   GR SD 938708

Situation and access

Blue Scar forms a crag of deceptive size and quality which lies a few hundred yards south-west of the road which runs through Littondale, half a mile or so south of Arncliff. The easiest approach is via the B6256 out of Skipton towards Grassington; and then take the B6160 Kettlewell road where the former reaches Threshfield. Pass the unmistakable Kilnsey Crag and fork left at the next junction towards Arncliff. After about 1½ miles, the crag can be seen up to the left, behind a farm (limited parking near here). Please

AT(56–58), Attermire Scar, The Escarpment

BS(1–7), Blue Scar

always ask permission at the farm before visiting the crag, and note that climbing is not allowed between March and some time in July to prevent disturbance to nesting birds. The most suitable route to the crag is by following the left side of a fence some 50 yards left of the farm buildings.

Character
This is a north-east facing crag, and as such displays all that is good and bad about such locations. It can be a cold and damp place to climb, but it also provides a welcome retreat from hot afternoon sunshine. Though the crag is divided into two tiers, the routes described are exclusively on the lower of the two, and are mostly of a high order of difficulty, being frequently both technical and bold.

The climbs
These are described from left to right.

At the very left-hand end of the lower tier of the crag is a right leaning overlap.

BS 1 **Blue Thunder**   19m   E3   5c
> 8m right of the overlap is a line of vague cracks. Climb these and continue direct to an abseil descent.

BS 2 **Some Blue For You**   19m   E1   5b   *
> A nice pitch starting at a groove a short way right from the last route. Climb the groove to a break, and ascend the wall above boldly to another break and a peg belay. Abseil off.

BS 3 **The Kill**   25m   E3   5c
> Right of the last routes is a grey wall containing a left-facing hanging groove. Climb this and leave it with difficulty to gain a break and peg runner. Continue up the wall above to a cave, tree and abseil.

BS 4 **Unreal**   24m   E3   6a   *
> Right of The Kill is a corner and 5m right of this is a series of slim and discontinuous cracks. Climb to a niche at the first break and continue up a faint line, moving rightwards near the top via flakes.

BS 5 **Blue Grit**   20m   E4   6a
> Start just right of Unreal and climb diagonally rightwards to a break, via a thread. Stand on a rock projection and ascend a slab to a peg. Continue via a flake and finish as for Unreal.

BS 6 **The Shootist**   19m   E5   6b   **
> Start a couple of metres left of a tree at the right of the wall. Climb to the break and move left past a thread, surmounting an overhang on to a slab. Climb this and the ensuing scoop

BS(8–17), Blue Scar

to the next break (thread). Follow holds leftwards past another thread to gain safety. An impressive route which is sustained, but reasonably protected.

BS 7 **The Spineless** 20m E5 6b *
Climb to the first break as for The Shootist. Move right beneath a peg and sling and gain this by a difficult series of

moves. Gain a break and climb past a hole to a belay and abseil descent. Rather serious.

Moving further right, across the drystone wall is the centrepiece of the crag, the impressive Central Wall.

BS 8 **Hammerhead**   30m   E6   6b   *

Start at a small tree which is below the left-hand of two bushes which protrude from the break. Poor rock just right leads to good rock and a ledge of sorts. Move scarily up and left to the bush and ascend the groove above (possible rest up to the right). From the top of the groove, climb the wall up to the left to a break (peg). A crack up on the right then leads to the top. Overall, a route of continuous difficulty and interest.

BS 9 **Priapism**   30m   E5   6b   ***

A stiff route up the wall between Hammerhead and Central Wall. Start right of Hammerhead, as for Central Wall. Climb leftwards up the wall, passing a brace of pegs, to a thread and peg at the break. Go directly up to the rest on Hammerhead; pass a thread and two pegs above. Continue directly, passing a peg on the left to a tree. Abseil descent.

BS 10 **Central Wall**   32m   E5   6a   **

A classic frightener. Start at a peg belay a few metres right of Hammerhead at the foot of a grassy groove. Climb this and gain a hand rail, which is eventually stood on after a series of moves left, up and back right. Move up into a flake crack on the left and then climb rightwards past a peg to a bush in the break (which is worth two on the ground). There is some ageing fixed gear up to the right here. Get above the bush and move left into a vague groove which is followed to a ledge. Swing over the ensuing bulge on the left and cross the final roof to a groove (peg) and finish to the right. Abseil descent.

BS 11 **Death Wish**   38m   E7   6b   ***

A highly serious route and a genuine classic which requires more than strong fingers. Start by following Central Wall to the bush and clipping the old fixed gear. Step down and hand traverse the break rightwards for a couple of metres when a step back up and a traverse right leads to a short corner and a poor in-situ nut. Move up and slightly right to gain the second break and swing right from here to a short corner. The right-hand wall leads to welcome trees.

BS 12 **Barracuda**   25m   E6   6b   *

Start immediately left of a large tree at the foot of the wall, at an old peg. Trend rightwards to the first break. Traverse left and follow a diagonal flake to the bush on Central Wall. Step right and ascend the wall and groove in a direct line, passing a couple of threads to a sharp finish.

BS 13 **Stairway to Heaven**   25m   E6   6c   ***

Another classic, though with better protection than some of its neighbours. Start as for Barracuda. Climb to the first break and step right passing a thread. Embark upon a desperate series of moves up the wall above, passing a bolt runner to the break with great difficulty. A long and bold section now leads rightwards up a ramp to the topmost break. Traverse left here to finish up Death Wish.

BS 14 **The Great White**   25m   E6   6b   ***

Start at a peg belay just right of the tree. Climb up to the left end of the roof (thread) and cross it, continuing to the horizontal break and peg runner. Move a metre left and aim for a tiny overlap. Climb the groove on its right past a thread and make an awkward exit left to the top break (peg and thread). Move up and right to the top via a satisfying jug. Abseil descent.

BS 15 **Blue Water White Death**   28m   E6   6c   ***
Yet another technically impressive route, again a daunting
proposition. Climb The Great White to the peg in the break
above the lower roof. Traverse 4m to the right here and
ascend a thin flake crack. Continue up the wall above to the
second break and continue rightwards above here, making a
controlled dyno/wild lunge for a bush. Abseil off.

BS 16 **The Underlap**   38m   E5   6a
Start a few metres left of a line of bolts which splits the
centre of the wall to the right. Gain a tree in the first break;
move right to a thread and climb straight up to the next
break with difficulty. Follow the overlap (threads) and finish
up a groove at its end. Tree abseil.

BS 17 **Professor of Desire**   22m   E6   6b   ***
A magnificent route taking the centre of the wall. Follow the
line of bolts to its end and move left and up to the break
(thread). Gain the next break (thread), and traverse right
past a peg to another thread. Continue up (thread) and
continue past a final peg to an abseil station.

Crummackdale   GR SD 783704

Situation and access
The crag lies high on the fell above the hamlet of Wharfe, which in
turn is just off the Horton-in-Ribblesdale road a mile or so north-
west of Austwick. A number of small parking areas can be found
near the two access roads to Wharfe (no parking in the hamlet).
Walk into Wharfe and take a bridleway which leads away up the
dale. Pass a couple of barns and go over a stone stile just before a
metal gate on the right. Follow the wall adjacent to the bridleway
into another field from where it is possible to strike up to the crag
more or less directly. Please contact the landowner, Mr Morphet on

Clapham 2880, before climbing here to ask permission as a matter of courtesy: the crag is not approachable by a public right of way.

Character
This is a crag with a dual character. It faces west and has an open and sunny aspect with wonderful views, good beer nearby and a selection of excellent routes. On closer inspection, however, the rock reveals a distinct lack of definite lines, especially those with an abundance of protection, and it has a reputation for seriousness. The latest protection techniques have made things a bit safer here, but steadiness will normally be found a better attribute than the ability to perform wild dynos.

The climbs
These are described from right to left. A stone wall meets the crag towards the right-hand side and provides a good reference point.

CK 1 **Epicure** 20m VS 5a
9m right of the stone wall is a corner holding a tree. Root a way past this to the roof, branch left and pull over. A good route for budding HVS leaders.

CK 2 **Feeling the Pinch** 18m E1 5b *
Start 5m right of the wall below a pinch which is easily located but not so easily let go. Gain the ledge and follow a direct line through the roof with difficulty.

CK 3 **The Unknown Dissident** 18m E4 6b **
Start just left of the wall and clip a peg a short way up. Move up left to join the traverse of Brothers and clip the peg in the roof (on Sha Sha a Gleneagles). Right is a little crack and an undercut. Traverse to these and hope that you're on good form for the next move.

CK, Crummackdale, Venus

CK (1–6)

CK 4 **Sha Sha a Gleneagles**   26m   E3   6b   *

CK 5 **Brothers**   25m   E2   5c   *

An entertaining climb following a line which is either illogical or entirely reasonable, depending on how hard you are finding the roof. Start by climbing some flakes 6m left of the stone wall, rightwards until an obvious traverse line is reached under the roof. Edge rightwards along this (remembering that this was originally standard VS), for 6m or so to a peg underneath the roof. Boldly go where plenty of others have already been, over the roof to a gentle finish.

CK 6 **Snowcem**   20m   VS   4b

Further left can be found the most attractive piece of rock here, a slab with a fine trilogy of routes, identified by the obvious right-slanting line of Venus. The following two routes start at a flake system which gives access to the slab towards its left-hand side.

CK 7 **Venus**   32m   VS   4c   ***

Up the flakes easily to a small ledge. Delightful balance climbing rightwards along the fault line leads to a corner just past some good underclings. Up steeply to easier ground.

CK 8 **Olympus**   30m   VS   4c   ***

Climb to the little ledge as for the last route. Step left on to the slab (thread) and ascend to a steepening. Ease daintily right to a big hold. Rock up and trend left to finish. Smart.

CK 9 **Little Pink Clare**   21m   HVS   **

Start under a triangular roof a few metres right of the start of Venus. Surmount this and climb in a pretty direct line via two undercling sections. Technically inspiring.

CK(1–6), Crummackdale

CK(7–12), Crummackdale

CK 10 **Jaywalk** 45m HVS 5a *

CK 11 **Arc of a Diver** 19m E1 5b

CK 12 **Norwester** 23m VS 5a

At the very left end of the crag is a steep wall with quite a bit
of fixed gear.

CK 13 **Motherspride** 21m E3 5c

CK 14 **Oystercatchers** 21m E4 5c

CK 15 **Bulk Order** 25m E5 6b **
Start under a conspicuous in situ thread 3m up. From this

CK(13–16), Crummackdale

move up right to a peg and continue up the wall via another peg runner. Steep and technical.

CK 16 **Bulk Delivery** 24m   E4   6a   *
Climb up to and past a jutting block 6m right of the last route. Move left and go more or less straight up.

Giggleswick Scars
There are two main climbing areas here, one at either side of the summit of Buckhaw Brow, the long hill 2 miles north-west of Settle.

GGS (1–9)

Giggleswick Scar South   GR SD 800658

Situation and access
This scar lies just south of the summit of Buckhaw Brow. The high-level crag on which lie the routes described can be seen above the woods on the right-hand side of the road as one approaches the Brow from Settle. The easiest approach is to park opposite the garage on Buckhaw Brow and follow a path which leads first up on to the fell and then turns right, crossing two stiles. The crag lies down on the right near a point where a couple of small caves can be seen in a scar on the left.

Character
Despite it being a fairly high-level crag, climbing is possible at most times of the year due to a sunny aspect and a quick-drying nature. The rock is normally excellent apart from the few obligatory loose sections near the crag top and most of the routes are in the upper grades, with the climbing being open, but generally steep.

The climbs
These are described from left to right.

GGS 1 **Yew Tree Rib**   11m   VS   4c
Start left of a short rib. At about 5m, move right to a small ledge and climb the groove to a tree.

GGS 2 **Pinnacle Direct**   11m   VS   4c
Climb a pinnacle between two yew trees and continue up the wall above.

GGS 3 **February Wall**   13m   VS   4c   *
Start 3m past the right-hand yew and get into a corner a few metres up via a stiff pull. Move on to the left wall and continue past an old tree.

GGS(1–9), Giggleswick Scar, South

GGS(10–15), Giggleswick Scar, South

GGS 4 **Broad Sword** 19m E3 5c **
Climb a groove to gain an undercutting traverse line and
continue up the groove right of the bolt. A direct finish is
possible at the same grade, climbing direct from the good
hold found before the undercut traverse.

GGS 5 **Mutton Dagger** 18m E2 5c ***
A testing route with fingery climbing and long reaches.
Climb a flake (thread runner) to some long stretches which
give access to a jug (junction with Broad Sword). Finish left
of the bolt.

GGS 6 **Prime Cut** 16m E1 5b *
From several metres up Mutton Dagger, move right to a
small niche and an ensuing groove line.

GGS 7 **Mint Sauce** 17m E1 5c
Gain a groove just left of the arete via a short wall, and
follow it to the top.

GGS 8 **Sir Loin** 18m E1 5c *
The arete is started with difficulty. From the ledge, follow a
line leading left to the top of Prime Cut.

GGS 9 **Little Corner** 15m VS 4c
A nice route up the crack in the right-facing corner.

GGS 10 **The Arches** E1 5c *
A good technical problem taking the arched overlap direct.
One of those routes which seem easy if you get them right,
but can be frustrating if you don't.

GGS 11 **Meerschaum** HVS 5b **
Climb the corner/groove system about 3m right of The
Arches. Quite strenuous and with some interesting moves.

GGS 12 **Satori** 12m HVS 5b
An obvious flake crack several metres right is gained from
the right.

GGS 13 **Power Pinch** 16m E3 6b *
The desperate thin crack and sustained wall above provide
technical and strenuous climbing.

GGS 14 **Orient Express** 19m E2 5c
The technical wall to the right leads to a break. Traverse left
for 4m and pull through a small bulge to finish up some
flakes.

GGS 15 **Go Johnny Go**   16m   E2   5c   *

As for the last route but follow the thin crack above the first
section, using holds to the right.

Giggleswick Scar North   GR SD 787663

Situation and access

The crag is situated immediately above the A65 road, just north of
Buckhow Brow. Park in a lay-by just over the top of the hill and on
the right as one travels north. The first buttress lies above the lay-by
and just to the left of a stone wall. It can be reached by a dodgy
move over an old barbed wire fence and a short uphill stroll.

Character

The crags lie in woods just above the road and are composed of a
number of distinct buttresses. The routes are very varied both in
length and in quality and those described are the pick of the bunch.
Facing south-west, the crag is quite sheltered, though its woodland
setting can give a vegetated and damp atmosphere.

The climbs

These are described from right to left. The first buttress is steep and
contains on its right-hand side a wide crack which suddenly
narrows.

GGN 1 **Red Rag**   15m   E1   5c

The wide crack, then a difficult move to gain the steep upper
wall.

GGN 2 **Broken Flake Wall**   15m   VS   4c

Ascends the wall just left of the crack.

The next climbs are on Hollywood Bowl, an impressive
feature reached by passing a couple of smaller crags.

GGN 3 **Hollywood Bowl**   26m   E5   6b   6c   *
1. 13m 6b. From the back of the Bowl, gain the cave via the rough line of some bolts.
2. 13m 6c. The left-hand wall of the cave and out through the roof, desperately, to the mere vertical.

GGN 4 **The Brink**   22m   VS   4b
Follows a line on the left edge of the cave, starting behind a tree on the left of the Bowl. Stand on a block at 5m, go to the lip and follow a groove to a small tree. Follow the wall and corner above. Continuing left, a short clean buttress can be found just before a stone wall.

GGN 5 **Soft Touch**   18m   E2   5c   *
The slim right-facing groove to a thread. Another hard move then leads to a loose finish.

GGN 6 **Fellsman**   18m   E1   5c
The wall just to the left. (In situ wire at the time of writing.)

Over the wall and about 100m further on is a higher buttress, whose base is rather obscured by trees and shrubs. A small ledge runs along its foot.

GGN 7 **Jackdaw Hole**   16m   E2   5c   *
Start by a yew tree at the right end of the wall and gain the hole from the right with difficulty. (Not advisable in the nesting season.) Move up and right to a small tree and finish direct.

GGN 8 **Mainlining**   16m   E5   6b
7m left of the Jackdaw Hole is a boss of rock. Climb to a peg in the bulge above this and aim for a peg with a sling on up to the right. Trend left from this to a thread and climb the wall above.

GGN 9 **The Ramp**   26m   E2   5c   **

A short wall gives access to a right- to left-slanting gangway. From the end of this, a hard move round the rib leads to easier ground. Continuously interesting climbing.

Further left is the most impressive buttress of the crag.

GGN 10 **Goldilocks**   30m   VS   4b   4b

Right of the highest part of the crag is a wall with a yew tree at half-height.
1. 13m 4b. A clean groove to the tree.
2. 17m 4b. The wall above to a tree-covered ledge, step right and move up to easier ground.

GGN 11 **Acid Test**   30m   E4   6b   **

Climb easy rock in the centre of the highest buttress to a ledge below a hairline crack. Thin and technical climbing leads to a break. Finish up the easier line above, tackling the final bulge direct.

GGN 12 **Ivy Buttress**   27m   E2   5c   *

1. 16m 5c. Start as for Acid Test, but move left off the easy wall to a ledge, via a bulge and peg. Ascend the peg-scarred crack to the left and belay just above a tree.
2. 11m 5a. The exposed and overhanging crack on the right.

GGN 13 **September Flake**   27m   HVS   5a

Gain the obvious flake crack to the left and follow it – continuously good.

Gordale Scar   GR SD 915642

Situation and access

Take the right fork in Malham village, over the bridge, and follow this small road past the Malham Tarn turning, until some parking

areas are reached at the bottom of a hill. A well-worn path leads
through level fields (camp site) into the gorge. One should be aware
of the dangers of rockfall to the hundreds of tourists who visit
Gordale, and it may not be wise to climb here at the busiest times
on routes which could cause this problem. There is also the
possibility of restrictions between March and July owing to nesting
birds – check with the National Park Authority's information centre
at Malham.

Character
An understandably popular tourist haunt, Gordale is a spectacular
and impressive place. Its towering walls and rushing waterfalls
create a unique atmosphere which many climbers prefer to savour
from the safety of the ground. The left-hand side of the gorge as one
approaches it receives most sunshine, whilst the big routes on the
right are in the gloom until later in the day.

The climbs

The Lower Left Wall

The climbs are described from left to right.

GO 1 **Scratchings** 11m   E1   5c
A stiff start gains an easier corner.

GO 2 **Nonsuch** 11m   E1   5c   *
Power up the flake crack.

GO 3 **The Eliminate** 26m   VS   4b   *
Climb a right-slanting slab to a flake and climb the right-
hand side of this to a corner and belay on a ledge a little
higher.

GO 4 **Tiptoe**   27m   VS   4c   4c   *
Start 5m right of the last route.
1. 12m 4c. Neat climbing up the corner to a ledge by a yew tree.
2. 15m 4c. Up from the tree is a corner. Climb this towards the roof and step right to avoid it on to a ledge. Straight up, then left to a slab and the top.

GO 5 **Overhanging Flake**   36m   VS   4b   5a
1. 18m 4b. The layback flake and crack to a stance.
2. 18m 5a. The clean wall above, keeping right of the tree.

GO 6 **Court Jester**   30m   E2   5c   *
Start at two cracks just left of a roof-topped corner. The cracks lead strenuously over the bulge. Get into the groove, climb to the roof and move round this to gain a ledge on the left. Have a rest and either belay or continue easily.

GO 7 **The Lyncher**   30m   E2   5c   *
An intimidating route which takes a recess a few metres right of Court Jester. Gain access to a block above the steep bit, move left past a dubious block and climb up to a crack which is followed to the top.

GO 8 **Yark**   29m   HVS   5a   5b   **
1. 15m 5a. Steeply out of the right of the cave into some grooves which lead to a recessed area and belay up to the right.
2. 14m 5b. A strenuous and scary pitch. Climb towards the overhang and wriggle into a chimney on its left. Up to the next roof which is pumpy, to a finish on the right.

The left wall of the gorge suddenly becomes much more impressive.

GO(1–8), Gordale Scar, Left Wall

GO (9-13)

GO 9 **The Cement Garden** 52m E6 6c *
Start at the large broken-looking corner which gets
progressively steeper as one approaches. Its right wall leads
past a bolt to a groove with a bolt to the right. Carry on up
the steep wall, past a doubtful peg to another bolt. Bypass
the roof above on the left and continue past an obvious break
via grooves to the top.

GO 10 **Face Route** 47m E3 5c 6a ***
A popular and established route of high quality.
1. 26m 5c. The relatively easy corner leads to exciting moves
round the roof by some flakes on the right which lead to a
welcome rest. The crack above leads to a well-pegged belay
in a cave.
2. 21m 6a. Move left into another cave and move up to yet
another. The next roof is hard, but well protected. A yew
tree provides a popular abseil descent.

GO 11 **Jenny Wren** 60m E4 5a 5c 6a *
Start at the foot of the towering arete.
1. 20m 5a. Fairly directly up the arete and wall past two
pegs to belay in the second cave.
2. 15m 5c. A worrying pitch which moves round to the left
and ascends a ramp which leads to the safety of the Face
Route belay.
3. 12m 6a. Another serious pitch which follows Face Route
to its crux roof which it avoids by a traverse left to a crack.
Climb this to a roof and climb the scary wall above to a
welcome finish.

GO 12 **Rebel** 47m E5 5a 6b 6a ***
1. 20m 5a. Pitch 1 of Jenny Wren.
2. 15m 6b. Step left to undercuts which lead to a groove and
a temporary respite. Continue to the roof and make a

GO(9–13), Gordale Scar, Left Wall

difficult traverse round to the left to a ledge. Easier climbing
leads up to a stance.
3. 12m 6a. Gaining the crack above can be frustrating. Once
gained, hurry up it to the top.

GO 13 **Girdle Traverse of the Left Wall**

138m   E2   5c   5b   5b   5b   5a   **

1. 36m. Climb any of the poor lines right of Yark to a
vegetated traverse right which ends with a belay on the last
tree. Not the best pitch on the crag, but things soon improve.
2. 21m 5c. Traverse at the same level for 5m and descend to
another traversing line which leads strenuously to a corner
and a stance on the rib on the right.
3. 12m 5b. The crack above leads to another traverse right
which leads to the yew tree on Face Route.
4. 9m. Move more easily rightwards to the cave belay on
Rebel.
5. 23m 5b. Descend a little and hand traverse right above
the corner and under the roof, continuing to gain a ledge.
Step back down to some more hard work rightwards and
gain an exposed stance on a prow of rock.
6. 8m 5b. Continue the traverse past a ledge which leads to
a stance.
7.   29m 5a. Gain a groove up to the left, surmount a bulge
and go past a pinnacle to some grassy ledges which lead up
to the left to a tree and a finish via a short groove on the
right.

The next climbs are on the right wall of the gorge and are
described from left to right.

GO 14 **Cabaret**   35m   HVS   5a   5a   *

A good route in a fine setting.
1. 20m 5a. Start by locating a small ledge on a rib above the
upper waterfall which is level with the obvious upper
horizontal break. Traverse this line to the right to a flake.

2. 15m 5a. Continue on the same line to finish up a corner.

GO 15 **Light**   35m   E1   5c   5a   ***
An impressive route up the steep wall which faces back
upstream. Though rather gloomy and frequently damp, it
provides a first-rate expedition.
1. 7m 5c. The safe, but overhanging and difficult crack.
2. 28m 5a. An impressive pitch. Leave the pinnacle with
trepidation and ascend a wall which leads to a neat corner
which is jammed to the roof. Move left and grovel into a
bottomless chimney which leads thankfully to easier
climbing.

GO 16 **Deliverance**   45m   E5   5c   6b   5c   ***
An amazing route which has a very intimidating
atmosphere.
1. 20m 5c. Start 2m right of Light. Summon up bags of
psyche and step on to the face on the right. Gain a crack and
follow it to a small roof which is climbed leftwards to a bolt.
The wall above leads to a break which is traversed
rightwards to a cave and belay.
2. 10m 6b. Up to a flake beneath an old bolt. Somehow
move past this to a flake which is followed excitingly to a
long reach for a pocket. Move left into a corner which leads
to a belay.
3. 15m 5c. Stand on an undercut ledge on the right, make a
difficult step left which leads to an easier crack and the top.
Wow!

GO 17 **Ivy Groove**   50m   E3   5c   5b   *
The impressive groove right of the main overhang.
1. 31m 5c. Gain the groove from the left and climb it to
moves right at the overhang. Climb up to a niche, move
right and climb a corner to a ledge and belay.
2. 19m 5b. Traverse the slab to a ledge and old tree. Aim for
some more trees by heaving over the bulge left of a groove.

GO (17–22)

Complete the route by climbing the grooves on the right.

GO 18 **Cave Route Left-hand**   45m   E6   6c   6a   ***
A stunning route taking the left-hand of two awesome lines.
1. 30m 6c. The desperate crack leads to a move right into
the right-hand line, high up and at an in situ thread. Abseil
off, or
2. 15m 6a. A crack on the right leads into a scoop. Move left
to another crack and follow this to a cave. Finish rightwards
to a tree belay.

The wall left of this is Supercool E7 6c, another incredible
route.

GO 19 **Cave Route Right-hand**   50m   E6   6a   6a   ***
The right-hand line of the two gives an equally stunning and
slightly easier route.
1. 35m 6a. Very steep climbing to a niche a third of the way
up. Exit from this (crux) and follow the obvious line to the
stance.
2. Abseil off or as for pitch 2 of the Left-hand.

GO 20 **Defcon 3**   35m   E7   6c   ***
A line of bolts leading right from Cave Route Right-hand
after 9m gives a route of immense difficulty which comes
back into the belay for the Cave Routes under the top roofs.

GO 21 **Pierrepoint**   50m   E7   6c   6b   ***
Another unbelievable route up the wall right of Cave Route
Right-hand.
1. 28m 6c. An overhanging crack to a small ledge on the left.
Right to a bolt, then up the crack desperately to a niche.
Move right then up and back left to a well-bolted belay.
2. 22m 6b. Climb to the bulge, and move rightwards round

GO(17–22), Gordale Scar, Right Wall

this to a resting place. Step right and complete the route up the fine rib.

GO 22 **Hangman** 60m E6 6b 6b 6a ***

1. 34m 6b. Climb Pierrepoint to the small ledge, then traverse right for 7m to a bolt belay.
2. 11m 6b. Up with difficulty to a point where a traverse left leads to a three-bolt belay under the bulge.
3. 15m 6a. Over the first roof with the obligatory difficulty and aim for a slim crack across and up to the right which leads to a tiny ledge. Step right and surmount an exposed nose to finish.

Great Close Scar GR SD 902667

Situation and access
This scar lies in a high and windswept position above Malham Tarn. It can be reached easily by following the Gordale road from Malham for a short way, before turning left up a small road signed to Malham Tarn. Follow this for about 2 miles to a large open grassy area where the road veers left and a barrier prevents vehicular access to the track which leads straight on. Park here and continue on foot until a short path up the scree leads to the foot of the crag (15 minutes). The crag is on land owned by the National Trust and it is an important nesting site. Climbing is therefore prohibited from the beginning of March until the end of June. As with all the crags in this guide, take care to keep other forms of disturbance to an absolute minimum.

Character
The crag is very much a continuous and steep buttress which is seamed with numerous crack and groove lines, mostly of good rock. Though the crag is exposed to winds, it does dry quickly, and facing south-west it attracts plenty of sunshine.

The climbs
These are described from left to right.

GC 1 **Gorm**   14m   HVS   5b
   The front of the left-hand buttress via a crack and a
   strenuous upper section through a bulge.

GC 2 **Mercenary Territory**   14m   HVS   5a
   A fair route up the wall right of the gully, moving rightwards
   through the bulge to gain the good upper wall.

GC 3 **Tarn Crack**   14m   MVS   4b

GC 4 **The Gibbet**   15m   HVS   5a

GC 5 **Hangman's Crack**   14m   VS   4c

GC 6 **Nomad**   17m   HVS   5a   *
   Good, open climbing up the centre of the attractive wall,
   passing a peg runner in the upper section.

GC 7 **Breakaway**   17m   HS

GC 8 **Bay Wall**   15m   HVS   5b
   Twin cracks in the back of the recess lead to a move up and
   right through bulging rocks to an easier finish.

GC 9 **President's Arete**   20m   HVS   5a   *

GC 10 **Sunshine Superman**   22m   VS   4c   *
   Weaves a line up a complex wall. Traverse right under the
   first roof, climb leftwards to the upper overhang and traverse
   left under this to finish.

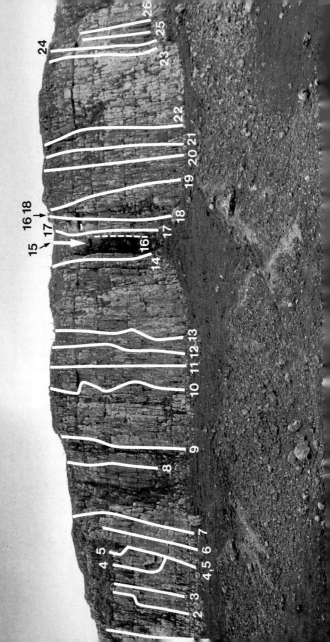

GC (1–26)

GC 11 **Black Death**   20m   E1   5b   *
The straight groove which forms a shallow chimney at half-height. Pleasant.

GC 12 **White Hope**   20m   E3   6a   *
Start 2m right of the last route and climb a line leading to a bulge and groove above. Climb rightwards to a gentler finish.

GC 13 **Fear of Flying**   20m   E1   5b
Start below a thin groove which widens to a slot. Up past this to an easier finish but on poor rock.

GC 14 **Quasimodo**   17m   VS   4c

GC 15 **Dolomite Rib**   11m   S
The juggy wall in the back of the gully.

GC 16 **Crossover**   24m   MVS   4b   *
Start on the left of the right wall of the gully. Climb a nose and make a rising traverse to the right-hand edge. Up, and then right under a roof to a groove.

GC 17 **Nectar**   19m   MVS   4b
A direct line up the arete on the right of the gully entrance.

GC 18 **Kestrel Wall**   24m   HS

GC 19 **Galleon**   22m   MVS   4b
The straight crack to a grassy finish.

GC 20 **Windjammer**   22m   MVS   4b   *
The next crack, which passes a small overhang at mid-height.

GC(1–26), Great Close Scar

GC 21 **Kayak** 22m VS 4c

GC 22 **Chibuku** 22m HS 4b
A clean-cut crack leads to a mediocre finish.

GC 23 **Fancy Bit** 20m HVS 5b *
From the foot of a left-slanting rake, pull through a bulge and move right into a little groove. Follow the edge of the wall to the top via a short crack high up. Nice climbing in an exposed situation.

GC 24 **Scimitar** 18m VS 4c *
One of the best known routes here, taking the curving crack in the corner.

GC 25 **Bitter Minnows** 17m E1 5c *
To the right is a steep wall seamed with cracks. Climb a protruding block of rock at its base and follow the thin cracks, moving right a little to reach the break. Continue up the corner crack above.

GC 26 **Scabbard** 17m HVS 5a *
An excellent route up a strong line in the right-hand side of the steep wall. Continue direct after the break.

Kilnsey Crag GR SD 974683

Situation and access
This monstrously overhanging crag cannot be missed as one drives along the B6160 Skipton to Buckden road near the hamlet of Kilnsey. There is parking in a lay-by a couple of hundred yards north of the crag and limited space near its south end. It is important that no agricultural access is blocked and that cars are parked so as not to obstruct traffic on the road. Climbing is

permitted on weekdays only and permission should be gained from the farm opposite the north end of the crag.

Character
The most obvious thing about Kilnsey is its uncompromising and neck-stretching steepness. All the routes are hard and strenuous and many of them would rank highly anywhere. There is nothing here for the lower-grade climber except inspiration, and the recent free ascent of the Main Overhang, along with other nearby routes, ranks as a real landmark in British climbing. Facing east, the crag provides welcome shade for a summer afternoon and a delightful early morning venue. Many routes have in situ gear, but local controversies have meant frequent changes in the state of some routes. Descriptions are as accurate as possible at the time of writing.

The climbs
These are described from left to right.

KC 1 **The Superdirectissima**   25m   E4   6a   **
Good climbing at a reasonable standard. Make a rising traverse left to gain what looks like a slab but feels like a wall. Continue up the thin groove and eventually move out right to a bolt belay.

KC 2 **Déja Vu**   25m   E4   6b   ***
Start below two in situ threads at 8m, half-way between the last route and a very obvious groove line – The Directissima. Gain the threads, up right to bolts and move down and right to a thread. Get into the groove and move left to a niche and bolt. Continue to a traverse line which leads left to a belay.

KC 3 **Wise Blood**   E6   6b   **
Either start as for Déja Vu and hurry left along a break at 5m, or start direct and follow a line left of it past peg runners.

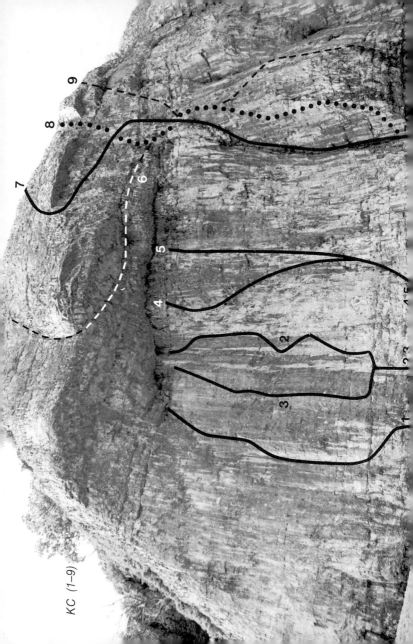

KC (1-9)

KC 4 **The Directissima** 25m E3 5c ***
An excellent pitch in its own right which follows the striking
line on the right side of the wall. Plenty of in situ gear and
sustained climbing leads to a belay and abseil point out to
the right beneath the roof.

KC 5 **Dream Time** 25m E6 6b ***
The groove right of The Directissima gives immaculate
climbing.

KC 6 **Mandela** 20m E8 6c ***
An incredible climb which frees the old aid route through the
main overhang. The line taken is the slanting crackline,
which gives more climbing than the size of the roof would
suggest. A truly outstanding achievement.

KC 7 **Lickerish** 75m E5 5c 6a 4b *
1. 30m 5c. Climb the impressive corner past a steepening
and climb its continuation to belay beneath the overhang.
2. 25m 6a. Directly up for 3m, then left and up past peg
runners to reach a break under the roof. Move left to a ledge
and climb a short wall past a peg to a small stance – nut
belays.
3. 20m 4b. Considerably easier climbing up and right to the
top.

KC 8 **Captain Trips** 52m E4 5c 6a ***
1. 35m 5c. Climb the corner for 3m and move right to the
arete passing a peg. Climb a groove in the arete and follow
the wall above to a cave. Traverse left to a stance.
2. 17m 6a. Attack the steep crack above and then move right
into a vague niche. Exit from this past a peg runner and
scurry right to good holds which lead to a finish.
An amazing route with plenty of strenuous variety.

KC(1–9), Kilnsey Crag

KC (7–13)

KC 9 **The Birdmen**   55m   E4   6b   5c   *
1. 30m 6b. An unbelievable pitch up the neck-ricking
crackline 12m right of the corner. Climb the crack past the
hole and continue passing a bush and a bolt to a series of
moves up and left to the cave on Captain Trips.
2. 25m 5c. Traverse right for 5m and climb a crackline
through some scary bulges which fortunately supply
reasonable holds.

Right of here is a smooth corner and right again is an
overhanging arete containing a groove.

KC 10 **Ground Effect**   25m   E5   6b   *
A difficult start gains this groove which is followed without
respite past threads until an easing allows a traverse up and
right to a belay and abseil point.

KC 11 **Balas**   30m   E4   6b   ***
The magnificent big corner across to the right gives a
sustained route of high quality. Ascend the corner (pegs)
until stopped by a bulge at 20m. Cross to the left past three
bolts and continue left to an abseil station.

KC 12 **Relax**   20m   E6   6b

KC 13 **Dihedral Wall**   25m   E5   6b   **
The impressive curving overlap is climbed with continuous
difficulty to a belay station shared with Relax.

Right from here is the wide, vegetated Central Gully.

KC 14 **Trauma Traverse**   107m   E2   5a   4c   5a   5b   5b   *
A genuine expedition.
1. 25m 5a. Climb the left-hand of two parallel cracks, pass a

KC(7–13), Kilnsey Crag

KC (14–20)

tree and move right to belay at another.
2. 22m 4c. Drop down and go right, grassily, to an arete.
Cross a bottomless groove to a ledge and peg belay.
3. 10m 5a. Move down and round the corner to a tree belay.
4. 25m 5b. Continue right in a sensational position to The
Diedre.
5. 25m 5b. Pitch 2 of The Diedre.

KC 15 **Bird's Nest Crack**   25m   E1   5b   *
Climb the crack right of the start of Trauma Traverse and
where this fades continue up the rib to the tree and an abseil
descent.

KC 16 **Zero Option**   35m   E6   6c   *
Climb the ramp line 15m left of the stone wall to a bolt at its
end. Move right into a short corner and climb up to a break
which is traversed rightwards until a move up leads to easier
terrain. Climb the wall leftwards past a couple of pegs to a
finishing crack, belay and abseil.

KC 17 **Central Wall**   50m   E4   6a   5a   ***
One of the best routes on Yorkshire limestone demanding a
positive attitude but giving immense satisfaction.
1. 35m 6a. Start at a point 10m right of the wall. Surmount
the overhang and climb the slanting slab up and left to a
peg. Move back right with difficulty, then up and left to a
rest. Continue up just left of some blocks and enter a groove.
Quit a small niche to the right and aim for the upper break.
Traverse this leftwards to a tree belay.
2. 15m 5a. The poor-looking groove or a convenient abseil.

KC 18 **White Rushin**   30m   E5   6b   *
Start as for the last route but climb directly through the

KC(14–20), Kilnsey Crag

KC (20–25)

bulge and follow a groove in the white streak to join the
Trauma Traverse. Traverse right to belay.

KC 19 **Claws** 65m E5 6a 6a ***
1. 35m 6a. Start as for The Diedre and after 3m traverse left
to a groove which leads to some big flakes. Trend left and up
to a traverse left which leads after 4m to a good foothold.
Aim for an easier groove up to the left which leads to a belay
on Trauma Traverse.
2. 30m 6a. Pass a bush up to the right and locate a good
thread above it. Go left and climb a scoop on unnatural
holds. Traverse the ensuing break for 3m leftwards and go
back right to the top via another scoop.

KC 20 **The Diedre** 50m E2 4c 5b ***
A magnificent line, traditionally graded HVS!
1. 25m 4c. The corner leads to a belay under the overhangs.
2. 25m 5b. Climb awkwardly up to under the first bulge and
move quickly over another bulge on the right into a groove.
(Good holds and a thread.) Make a hard move left to a small
ledge and climb up to the tree. Hand traverse right into the
corner which leads more easily to the top. A first-class pitch.

KC 21 **Worlds in Collision** 45m E3 5c 5b
1. 27m 5c. Climb The Diedre for 8m and traverse right until
a short groove in the arete leads to in situ gear. Gain a good
flake up to the left and continue left and then up to a good
ledge.
2. 18m 5b. Directly up to a thread, move right to a peg and
move up to reach undercut holds which lead into a groove to
finish.

KC(20–25), Kilnsey Crag

KC(11), Balas, Kilnsey Crag

KC 22 **Dominatrix**   25m   E6   6b   ***
   Climb the corner past two pegs and two threads and

continue past a bolt into a vague groove. Reach the next roof and surmount this rightwards to a bolt over the lip. Move left and up with difficulty to complete the route.

KC 23 The Thumb 45m E7 6c ***

An incredible route up the first big overlapping and left-slanting line. It was bolted up at the time of writing.

KC 24 The Overlap 35m E5 6b ***

Climb the corner and pull through the roof to a peg which is normally in place. Move up and left into another groove and follow this to its end (pegs). Make a move left then back right to a bolt belay.

KC 25 Little Ernie 27m E6 6c *

Start 4m left of a bottomless groove above the bulges at an undercut. Up to some in situ slings and swing right strenuously to gain the groove. Climb this past a bolt and move up into a niche. Yet another steep wall and roof lead eventually to a tree.

Loup Scar GR SE 029618

Situation and access
Park in the village of Burnsall and after crossing the bridge over the River Wharfe, follow its true left bank for about 500 yards to reach the crag, which is situated on a bend. Access may be curtailed when the river level is high for those without a boat.

Character
A sheltered and sunny crag, which is so steep it is nearly always dry. Virtually without exception, the routes are very strenuous, and at busy times a good audience of tourists is guaranteed.

LS (1-9)

The climbs
These are described from left to right.

LS 1 **Swing Time**   10m   E2   5c
Climb a short overhanging crack on the left of the crag and the groove above to the tree.

LS 2 **Guided Muscle**   10m   E4   6a

LS 3 **Loupy Lou**   25m   E3   6b
The wide roof crack with a hard pull around the lip.

LS 4 **Lapper**   22m   E2   5c   **
A ramp system can be seen in the upper part of the crag. Get on to this via a pillar and a crack, and follow it for 10m until a move through a bulge (peg runner) leads to a tree.

LS 5 **Guadaloupe**   25m   E5   6b   ***
As for the last route to start, but power across the huge roof instead of moving right.

LS 6 **Slapper**   18m   E4   6b

LS 7 **Slap Happy**   18m   E5   6a

LS 8 **Central Crack**   18m   E4   6c
Climb the steep crack in the centre of the crag to a roof. A tough exit left on to the ramp leads to a shared finish with Lapper.

LS 9 **Louper**   22m   E2   5b
As for Central Crack to the roof, then traverse right along the ramp and finish up the groove.

LS(1–9), Loup Scar

MC (CW)

The Right Wing

The Terrace

Main overhang

To Right Wing

Upper

Lower

The Central Wall

The Left Wing

The Catwalk

Path to Left Wing

Malham Cove   GR SD 897642

Situation and access

The mighty Malham Cove lies a mile and a half north of Malham village and can be seen from a variety of locations further south. Malham village is easily reached from the A65. From the south, and Skipton, turn right at Gargrave and go through Kirby Malham. From the north, turn left in Settle and follow the road over the moors to Kirby Malham. (This is the same road on which Attermire Scar is reached.)

In Malham village, there is plenty of parking available, but most climbers drive up the road some way (the left fork in the village), and park on the right near the farm, taking care not to cause any obstructions. A short stroll up the road leads to a very obvious and well-used path leading down right to the meadows and the Cove. The Left Wing is reached via some horrendous steps on the left, and the Right Wing by a steep path which now enters a small plantation.

Character

Malham is one of the most impressive and important crags in Britain. Although there are some sections of poorer rock, most of it is excellent and a joy to climb on. The Cove faces south and, due to its shape, it is usually possible to climb somewhere here throughout the year, though hot summer afternoons can be just a little too hot. Malham has always been a forcing ground, evolving as it has from its big aid route era right through to its present position at the forefront of British free climbing. Its recent past has been one of confusion and controversy, with some poorer routes being climbed, often short, heavily bolted and frequently forced into submission in a style of climbing far removed from the previous British norm. More recently, some truly amazing routes have been added – perhaps these will put things into perspective. The excellent Yorkshire

MC, Malham Cove

Limestone guidebook and supplement are recommended to those seeking fuller details of the cluster of hard routes put up over the last few years which are not included here. Although Malham has virtually nothing for the low-grade climber, those climbing above VS will find plenty to enjoy.

The climbs
These are described in separate sections, beginning with climbs on the Central Wall which start from the Catwalk.

The Central Wall

This incredible bulk of overhanging rock now has a complete route up its centre – a free climb representing the modern idiom in every way and impressive by any standards. Other routes are starting to overcome the capping roofs and it will be interesting to see how popular these very difficult problems become. The other routes are all steep and hard, and the lower sections of this wall contain many routes which follow bolt ladders, often giving an atmosphere of intensity and competition which some hate and others love.

It should be remembered that most of these routes are 'dogged' into submission, and on-sight flash ascents of the harder routes are rare. The first route starts 10m from the left end of the wall at a line of undercut flakes.

MC 1 **Yosemite Wall**   36m   E5   6a   .***
The flakes lead rightwards to low moves avoiding the steep little hanging corner. Continue up the flake to the roof and go right to an abseil chain.

MC 2 **Tremolo**   23m   E6   6b   **
Starts 8m right of Yosemite Wall and initially follows the

MC(1–10), Malham Cove, The Central Wall, Lower Section

line of a thread and three bolts. Follow a groove line on the right of a shield of rock and 3m above this aim across to the belay of Yosemite Wall. Bold and sustained.

MC 3 **Mescalito**   27m   E6   6b   ***
Another awesome route which starts 2m left of New Dawn and ascends a not very obvious groove and flake line to rejoin that route. Follow New Dawn through the bulge and from the 'rest point' aim for an undercut to the left. A devious move left just before this leads to an abseil descent from in situ gear in Yosemite Wall.

MC 4 **New Dawn**   27m   E6   6c   ***
A stupendous route attacking very steep ground. Start at the remains of an old bolt and a pock-marked stalactite a couple of metres up. Climb past this and up to a seriously bulging section. Undercling boldly leftwards to finish at Yosemite Wall's abseil chain.

MC 5 **Zoolook**   32m   E7   6c   ***
Start 5m right of New Dawn where a comforting flake can be reached only by a desperate move or by a Harlem Globetrotter. Follow a line up to the right past a peg in the foot of a groove to a relatively small but difficult roof. Hard and intricate climbing leads to an abseil point. The roof above is now climbed by The Well Dunne Finish, raising the overall grade slightly.

MC 6 **Cry Freedom**   25m   E9   7a   ***
A line based on the old aid route controversy, which demanded a long siege for success, and which at the time of its ascent was rated as one of the hardest routes in the world.

MC(1–14), Malham Cove, The Central Wall, Lower Section

MC 7   **Le Maximum**   15m   E7   6c   **
Start at some flakes beneath a bulge 6m right of Zoolook and
follow a line of bolts, usually very intermittently.

MC 8   **Overnight Sensation**   15m   E7   6c   *
The very bulging wall which used to be aided as Piggy Bank
Wall.

MC 9   **The Austrian Oak**   15m   E8   7a   *
A very difficult line which trends rightwards.

The next routes start below a prominent curving undercut
flake across to the right and about half-way up the wall.

MC 10   **Chiselling the Dragon**   12m   E5   6c   *
A difficult start past the cluster of old bolts which mark the
start of the old Directissima aid route may lead to the left
side of the undercling. Continue to an abseil point.

MC 11   **The Seventh Aardvark**   12m   E5   6b   *
A line past the right side of the undercut.

MC 12   **Rated PG**   E5   6a   *
An unusually serious route for this part of the crag. Hard
moves gain an undercut 3m up (wire just above this).
Increasingly scary climbing up and right to bolts and the
usual descent.

MC 13   **Consenting Adults**   E5   6a   *
Climb more or less direct to the abseil point on Rated PG.

MC 14   **Totally Free**   83m   E9   7a   ***
An outstanding free climb up the full length of the wall
which must have been the dream of so many. Originally

MC(9–16), Malham Cove, The Austrian Oak

climbed as one pitch, its established format has not yet been rationalised, but it is destined to become a world classic.

MC 15 **Free 'n' Even Easier** 12m E5 6a *
Starts at a smattering of bolts below and left of a break in the roof.

MC 16 **Bongo Fury** 12m E5 6c **
Start 2m right below a big side pull and follow bolts.

About 20m right is

MC 17 **Bolt Revolt** E3 6a *
A rising leftwards traverse past two threads and a peg provides pleasant and balancy climbing. Another thread leads to a tiny overhang. Move over this and pass another peg on the way to the abseil point.

The whole of the lower wall just described is still undergoing development and a number of bolted lines will be forced other than those described. Friendly locals will normally provide the necessary information.

The Right Wing

The next sections described are the Right Wing and the right-hand upper side of the Central Wall where a good variety of quality routes of all grades except the easiest can be found. The Right Wing, with its excellent rock and fine routes, is the most popular part of the crag. The climbs are described from right to left, beginning about 20m left of a fence which meets the right end of the Wing.

MC 18 **Lightning Crack** 13m VS 5a

MC 19 **Swingover** 15m VS 5a

MC 20 **Clubfoot** 18m VS *
A varied route starting at a corner/groove a couple of metres
right of a tree 5m up the crag. A few moves up lead to a
delicate toe traverse left to the tree. Complete the route via
the crack to its left.

MC 21 **Olaf** 18m HVS 5a *

MC 22 **Overhanging Crack** 19m HVS 5a

MC 23 **Vertical Crack** 19m E2 5c

MC 24 **Pikedaw Wall** 20m HVS 5a **
A fine climb. From a niche in the left-facing groove, move
right and up on excellent holds and aim for the tree. The
slender crack to its right concludes the route.

MC 25 **Daytona** 19m E3 5c

MC 26 **Friday the 13th** 20m E3 6a *

MC 27 **The Cavern** 24m HVS 5b 5a
1. 12m 5b. A vague ramp leads rightwards to a stiff pull
round the overhang and into a cave.
2. 12m 5a. Move up steeply into a niche and sidle right to
an easier groove. A varied and worthwhile climb.

The next routes share a start at the left end of a shallow
cave.

MC 28 **The Kylin** 26m HVS 5b 4c *
1. 13m 5b. A rather polished start gains a jug. Follow the
groove on the right to the overhang and go right to the large
vegetated ledge.
2. 13m 4c. Ascend a ramp line which cuts back left and top
out via an easy crack.

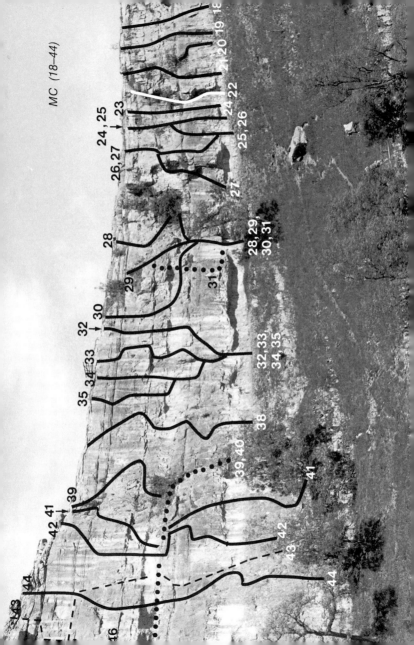

MC (18–44)

MC 29 **Junkyard Angel**   24m   HVS   5b   *
Follow the last route to the overhang, then move over this
and climb diagonally leftwards to the top.

MC 30 **Kirby Wall**   30m   HVS   5b   4c   ***
A great climb, full of character.
1. 14m 5b. As for the last two routes to the roof. A lovely
traverse left gains a welcome ledge.
2. 16m 4c. Wander left to a ledge reached after 5m. The
flake leads to a move right, a wall and a final corner to round
off a very satisfying excursion.

MC 31 **Cathay Pacific**   26m   E4   5c   6a

Another set of routes share a polished start 25m left, at the
end of an undercut section.

MC 32 **Regatta de Blanc**   27m   E5   6a   *
An exciting route starting up the polished wall and breaking
out right to reach a scoop which leads to a roof. Ascend this
and the ensuing flake and finish up a shallow crack and
corner on the right.

MC 33 **Wombat**   27m   E2   5c   ***
A brilliant line, sustained and varied. Climb the wall and
corner above, moving right on to a sloping ledge. Up to the
roof, sneak round this on the right (peg) and climb the
corner above to a wobble left at its end. Power up the final
wall to a fencepost belay.

MC 34 **Doubting Thomas**   27m   E5   6a   ***
Another mega-classic. Climb the polished wall and make a
couple of moves up the grooves above this. Traverse gently
left and then up to a sloping ledge and an old bolt. Climb

MC(18–44), Malham Cove, The Right Wing

past the left-hand side of the roof and continue direct via a crack and difficult wall to an easy finish.

MC 35 **Slender Loris** 28m E3 6a ***

Yet another great route, offering sustained and strenuous climbing. Climb Doubting Thomas to the old bolt. Move left and follow a flake on to a ramp. Up this to a break, and finish to the right via a peg.

MC 36 **East Wall Route** 42m E2 5c 5a *

1. 18m 5c. Climb the wall and move left to a peg. Go down and left to a good hold and continue left to a tree.
2. 24m 5a. Balancy climbing left for 5m and a short wall leads to a left-leaning gangway, up which the route finishes.

MC 37 **Wind and Wuthering** 29m E3 6a *

MC 38 **Crossbones** 29m E2 5b 5c ***

Start below and just left of an obvious tree belay 12m up.
1. 12m 5b. Climb to a sapling at 3m and move up and across right to the tree on good rock.
2. 17m 5c. The short wall above the belay is not easy, but leads to a step right and the beautiful finishing gangway.

MC 39 **Scorpio** 31m HVS 5a 4c *

1. 13m 5a. The corner leads to a small tree. Move left on to a slab and take a stance at the left end of the ledge.
2. 18m 4c. Move up, then traverse right and climb the left trending gangway.

MC 40 **Carnage Left-Hand** 60m E2 5a 5b 6b (5b with 1pt aid) ***

A very popular and well-known route which is normally climbed with a point of aid on the start of the top pitch, when it is E1 5b.
1. 14m 5a. As for Scorpio.

2. 27m 5b. Climb down to a tree on the left and reascend to
gain a technical leftwards traverse which eventually reaches
another ledge and tree belay (junction with Carnage).
3. 19m 6b. Move right and pull over the roof with great
difficulty or at a more amenable 5b making use of the peg.
The steep wall leads to a break. Hand traverse left to gain
access to a corner which is followed to a step left and the
final arete.

A lower wall can be found to the left, which appears more
broken and has a number of trees at its foot.

MC 41 **Seventh Grade**   45m   E5   6b   6a   **
Start behind the second tree.
1. 21m 6b. Trend left to a small tree. Up to the right is a
ledge and bolt runner: from this, tackle the bulge with great
difficulty.
2. 24m 6a. A short corner leads to the left end of a roof.
Move right over this and climb a groove to a horizontal
break. Swing to the right to an easier finish.

MC 42 **El Coronel**   46m   E6   6a   6b   ***
Start behind the dead tree, which will one day be the old
stump.
1. 22m 6a. Aim for a good flake at 8m. Slightly left, then
right to a downwards-pointing flake. The groove above leads
to a break, a traverse right and a hard move on to the ledge.
2. 24m 6b. Traverse left and climb a steep bulge to a groove.
Follow this, then gradually trend right to finish.

MC 43 **Mulatto Wall**   48m   E3   5c   5b   **
Start behind an ash tree, 3m left of the last route.
1. 24m 5c. Broken rock leads to a groove. Follow this past its
end via pockets and an old bolt to an easier section which
leads leftwards to a large ledge.
2. 24m 5b. Move back right to beneath a hanging corner.

Climb this and the ensuing crack to a welcoming ledge. Go left and finish as for Carnage.

MC 44 **More Monkey than Funky** 45m E5 5c 6b
1. 23m 5c. The right-hand of two thin cracks leads past a peg to junction with Mulatto Wall. A sloping ledge 3m higher provides an adequate stance.
2. 22m 6b. Continue directly through the roof, peg runner, then up a groove and final difficult wall. A strenuous and thought-provoking pitch.

MC 45 **Chasing the Dragon** 46m E5 6a 6b **
1. 22m 6a. The left-hand crack to a move right on to a sloping ledge and thread. Go left through the bulge and climb a short groove, gaining the belay ledge via the steep slab.
2. 24m 6b. Move right and climb the Carnage roof to a break. Climb up and right to a hole, step right and trend leftwards up an impressive grey wall to another break. Move right and climb a short crack to the Carnage finish.

MC 46 **Carnage** 46m E2 5b 6b (5b with 1 pt of aid) ***
A well-established classic around which many other routes weave. Start behind a large ash, 5m left of the last route.
1. 23m 5b. Get on to the ledge and climb rightwards through the bulge. Continue up and right to the dark bulge above, at which level a traverse left leads to a peg runner. Climb past the small tree above, rightwards to a tree belay.
2. 23m 6b. Move right and climb the roof, normally at 5b using the peg. Up the wall to a break. Traverse right here and climb a short crack to the well-photographed Carnage mantelshelf, which may not be all it appears. Move up and right to finish.

From this point, it is possible to continue on to the Central Wall via a ledge system which gradually peters out. The routes on this section are described from right to left.

MC 47 **Gorgon Direct** 25m E5 6b **

Start below a pillar 15m up. A series of cracks, flakes and pockets lead up to the pillar via bolt runners. Cross the pillar to the left to a ledge and move back on to its front to finish over the exposed roof.

MC 48 **The Seventh Toad** 19m E5 6b **

Start a couple of metres left of the last climb. A very taxing route which gives little respite. Thin flakes lead to a bolt. Move right to a good hold and aim for an undercut (threads). Continue straight up, then leftwards to a hard ending.

MC 49 **The Main Overhang** 36m E6 6c and A2 ***

1. 18m 6c. This line of the bolt ladder beneath the widest part of the roof leads to a niche. This can still be aided to give access to the big second pitch.
2. 18m A2. A popular and sensationally exposed roof.

MC 50 **Herbie** 20m E6 6b **

Left of The Main Overhang are three 'elephant's trunks'. Start beneath the right-hand one and somehow gain and climb it to a bolt belay.

MC 51 **Obsession** 19m E6 6b ***

A popular test piece for aspiring supermen. Start 6m left of The Main Overhang at a double bolt belay. Follow a line of bolts with a move left after a few metres to gain the upper wall via a dark niche. A fingery and sustained pitch. (Aren't they all?)

MC 52 **Renaissance/Breach of the Peace** 35m E8 6c ***

A combination of two excellent pitches, culminating in a

wild roof. Renaissance can be climbed as a route in its own right at an overall grade lower.

MC 53 **L'Ob Session**   20m   E7   6b   ***
Another mega-route climbing the white wall 3m left of Obsession. Take six quick draws and strong fingers.

MC 54 **Free 'n' Easy**   25m   E6   5c   6c   ***
1. 5m 5c. From the end of the ledge, traverse left into an exposed position and reach a bolt belay at the foot of an old bolt ladder – the second pitch of Totally Free.
2. 20m 6c. A free version of the aid route in a stunning position.

MC 55 **The Right Wing Girdle**
146m   E2   4c   5a   5c   5b   5b   5a   ***
Very worthwhile and highly enjoyable, but perhaps best on a quiet day. Start at Clubfoot.
1. 39m 4c. Climb Clubfoot to the tree and continue traversing left to the vegetated ledge on The Kylin.
2. 12m 5a. Move down and traverse left as for Kirby Wall to belay as for that route.
3. 39m 5c. Climb Kirby Wall to the small tree. Continue up the corner and make a series of moves leftwards to the peg on Wombat. Descend to join the East Wall Route and follow this to its tree belay. This pitch could be split.
4. 10m 5b. Continue by a hand traverse to a belay in the jungle as for Scorpio.
5. 27m 5b. As for Carnage Left-hand.
6. 19m 5a. Climb the belay tree and transfer from wood to rock. Move right and up to a horizontal break. Hand traverse left and ascend a corner which gives access to a leftwards finish at its top.

MC(47–54), Malham Cove, The Central Wall, Upper Section
MC(57–71), Malham Cove, The Terrace and Central Wall, Upper Section

MC 56 **Pumpwater Meets The Hulk**
105m   E4   5a   6b   6a   6a   ***
A sustained and powerful trip.
1. 27m 5a. Climb Scorpio to a good ledge 6m from the top,
or reach it from above.
2. 36m 6b. Go left round an arete to a short corner. Climb
down and veer left on some horizontal breaks and a small
pocket to a welcome ramp. Continue left to below the
ubiquitous Carnage mantelshelf, step down and hand
traverse left round an arete to a small hawthorn. Now move
up and left to a tree belay.
3. 30m 6a. Descend and hand traverse leftwards along a
break to join New Dawn Fades. Downclimb its groove and
go left to the bottom of the ramp of Midnight Cowboy. Up
this to the flake and then move stealthily left past a groove to
a small tree and belay.
4. 12m 6a. Hand traverse the top break left to the thread on
Sundance Wall and complete the climb by finishing up this.

The Terrace

This is the exposed wall at the top of the Cove which is
reached from the left, where the ledge beneath it is at its
most comfortable size. The routes are for the most part on
excellent rock and many have an atmosphere and character
which timid climbers might not enjoy. The climbs are
described from left to right.

MC 57 **Letterbox Wall**   7m   S
The wall 3m left of the crack containing the tree.

MC 58 **Terrace Crack**   8m   VS   5b
A stiff move at 3m provides the meat. Beyond this, pass the
tree and climb the rest of the crack.

MC 59 **Problem Wall** 8m E1 6a
Gain a scoop via a testing start. Trend rightwards using
some breaks.

MC 60 **Cove Crack** 8m E2 6b
The wicked crack which rises out of the shallow cave.

MC 61 **Ivy Corner** 10m HS
A pleasant route climbing a wall and flake to gain the corner
5m right of the last route.

A scary step down leads to a lower level, from which the next
routes start.

MC 62 **Butch Cassidy** 15m E4 6b **
Climb into a corner which is topped by a roof, from the left.
Stretch up left to a short flake crack and finish direct up a
thin crack in the upper wall.

MC 63 **Black Dyke** 15m E2 5c *
3m right of the last route is a hanging groove which can be
reached by a hand traverse from the left. Layback the groove
to a well-positioned foothold. Grope left to a steady finish.

Just right is a shallow cave containing a huge thread.

MC 64 **Terrace Wall** 16m VS 5a **
A great route which every VS leader should do. A difficult
pull over the bulge 3m right of the thread leads to a break
and a traverse back left into the left slanting groove. Climb
this more reasonably past a small tree and exit left to extract
the maximum enjoyment from the situation.

MC 65 **Wild West Hero** 20m E5 6b ***
As for Terrace Wall to the break. From here, move right and
up to a good but small hold. Up to the right is a blunt and

pock-marked spike. Pass this with difficulty and reach a decent but elusive flake. Hand traverse a break leftwards to another flake and cruise the scoop to finish. Very attractive climbing.

MC 66 **Sundance Wall** 17m E2 5c **

An excellent and typically exposed climb. From a point where the ledge becomes disconcertingly non-existent, climb to a break and follow thin cracks and a short traverse right to an open groove. Up this passing an impressive thread.

MC 67 **Swift Attack** 19m E2 5c **

More excellent climbing which starts under a black groove 2m right of Sundance. Follow a flake crack at the end of the groove, rightwards to some comforting holds. A hard move up and right leads to an easier finish up a groove.

MC 68 **The Stone Tent** 18m E1 5c

A scary traverse leads to a narrow ledge and a tree belay. From behind the tree, gain the break and move left into a clean-cut groove. From the end of this, a thin crack completes a pleasant pitch.

MC 69 **Midnight Cowboy** 20m E3 5c ***

Start at a flake 6m right of the tree. Use this to reach a ramp which is followed daintily leftwards to a shake-out beneath the flake. Finish by this – a superb climb on immaculate rock.

MC 70 **New Dawn Fades** 24m E5 6b **

Start Midnight Cowboy, then move right and climb a broad groove leftwards to a little corner. Climb the steep wall with difficulty to some secretive pockets which lead right to a ledge. Stretch up left to a flat hold and pull up into a pleasant finishing groove.

MC, Malham Cove, The Main Overhang

MC 71 Limehill 30m E4 6a **

Start 8m right of the tree. A series of pockets leads to a break. Traverse right to an overhanging groove, climb this and leave it rightwards on flakes to reach a scoop. Aim for the tree up to the right.

MC(72–79), Malham Cove, Left Wing

The Left Wing

This is reached by a walk up the steps and a short rising traverse. The routes here are generally short, but some of them are excellent.

MC 72 **The Thistle** 8m VS 5b
The groove has a difficult start.

MC 73 **Th-rows** 8m HVS 5b
The steep undercut arete is gained via an undercut and climbed via a flake and a fluted section.

MC 74 **Crown of Thorns** 8m HVS 5b
A hanging flake reminiscent of many others.

MC 75 **Reluctant Passenger** E3 5c
A steep wall and crack, just right of the hawthorn.

MC 76 **Short Groove** 12m E2 5c
The hanging corner past the tree.

MC 77 **Rose Corner** 12m E4 6a
A hard series of underclings leads left to sustained laybacking up the next hanging groove.

MC 78 **The** 11m E2 5c *
The next groove line.

MC 79 **Stern** 8m VS 5a
The next reasonable-looking groove.

MC 80 **Cube Root** 11m E1 5b *
Nice climbing up the left side of the flake to a stiff heave through the bulge to finish.

MC 81 **Square Root** 11m VS 5a
Climb to the flake and move right into a crack, which is followed to final moves on the left.

MC 82 **Flake Wall** 10m S **
A groove leads to a flake on the left. Gain the ledge and finish to the left.

MC(80–90), Malham Cove, Left Wing

MC 83 **Rook**   9m   E1   5c

MC 84 **Chough**   9m   E1   6a
Undercut into a corner and exit right.

MC 85 **Original Route**   17m   S   **
A polished flake leads to a bulge and chimney. Fairly
strenuous, but enjoyable climbing.

MC 86 **Saplink**   18m   HVS   5b   *
Become ensconced on a sloping ledge a short way to the
right. Traverse left and go up to another ledge and climb the
corner above.

MC 87 **Warspite**   20m   E3   6a
Start under a roof and cross it via an undercling and large
flake. Carry on up and left to a good ledge (peg). Aim for a
tree on the left via a bulge and so to the top.

MC 88 **Going Dutch**   19m   E3   6a   *
From a standing position on the flake of Warspite, traverse

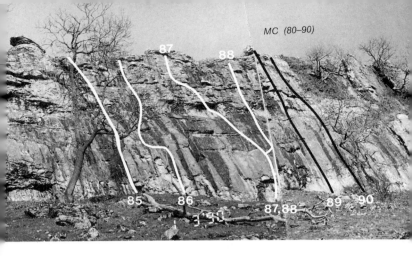

right and climb the wrinkled wall and its continuation.

MC 89 The Well-oiled Machine 21m E3 6a 6a
Start a couple of metres left of a large tree.
1. 10m 6a. A thin crack leads to the ledge and a belay across left.
2. 11m 6a. Move back right and ascend a steep white wall past a thread, and moving right beneath the top.

MC 90 Sarcophagus 21m E2 6a *
Climb a wrinkled brown wall behind the tree to a ledge. Step into a thin crack above from the right and ascend it to a peg. Hard moves left lead to another crack which provides an easy finish.

Upper Wall – Left-hand Side

MC 91 Local Hero 30m E8 6c ***
A free version of the top pitch of the Directissima aid climb. Originally finishing beneath the roof, it now surmounts this to give a very sustained pitch. Start at a bolt ladder behind the end tree.

PS (1–5)

Pot Scar   GR SD 795678

Situation and access

A sunny, south-facing crag above the hamlet of Feizor, which is 4 miles north-west of Settle, just off the A65. It is important that the following access arrangements are adhered to. Either park at Feizor Gap (reached by driving through Feizor and continuing through a gate and up a small road to a level area), or ask permission at the bungalow or converted barn to park in the enclosure on the opposite side of the road. Follow the track from the centre of Feizor which is signposted to Stainforth. Cross the field to a stile in the top right-hand corner, follow the wall round and strike up the hillside to the crag. Please do not climb walls when approaching or leaving the crag.

Character

Pot Scar is a friendly crag, with some good middle-grade routes, the central section being particularly attractive. An open, sunny aspect and a fine panorama complete the picture.

The climbs

Described from left to right, starting at an attractive, smooth wall on the left wing of the crag.

PS 1 **Meek and Mild**   12m   VS   4c

PS 2 **Herbivore**   14m   E1   5c
    The steep, crozzly wall on small holds.

PS 3 **Carnivore**   14m   E2   6a

PS 4 **Diagonal**   10m   E2   5c
    Another good, clean route which requires a dynamic approach.

PS(1–5), Pot Scar

PS (6-15)

14, 15

6 7 8 9 10 11 12 13

PS 5 **Block Gangway**   14m   D

The Main Crag

About 40m after some broken ground and a possible descent
route, is a better area of rock. The first route is identified by
a 4m long ledge, which ends up about 3m off the ground.

PS 6 **Cannabis**   15m   VS   4c
From the right end of the aforementioned ledge, climb
athletically to gain a ramp which leads up to a pinnacle on
the left. Stand on this and climb the short wall to finish.

PS 7 **Potholers' Proddle**   17m   VS   4c

PS 8 **Mort's Crack**   17m   VS   5a   *
A good route up the left-trending thin crack which emanates
from near the foot of Nirvana. The lower section is quite
awkward, but it eases to a finish either up the corner or the
rib on the right.

PS 9 **Nirvana**   17m   VS   4c   **
An excellent line up the deep groove, with a slight detour
right to ease past the bulge.

PS 10 **The Pusher**   17m   VS   4c   *
Just right is another groove, whose base fades into a steep
wall. Get into the groove from the right and either finish
direct, or traverse right into a pleasant scoop and finish up
this. Good climbing.

PS 11 **Addiction**   17m   VS   4c   *
Start 5m right of Nirvana, below an overlap. Climb to this
via a small groove and a thin crack. Up and left into the

PS(6–15), Pot Scar

scoop finish on The Pusher and ascend this or the rib on the right.

PS 12 **LSD** 18m E1 5b *
A hard start up a tiny groove and smooth wall, right of the last route, leads to the roof. Swing over this joyfully to a final steep wall which contains excellent holds.

PS 13 **Overdose** 17m VS 4c
A small groove and slab gain a flake. Go up and left, cross the bulge on jugs and top out via a corner and short wall. Quite pleasant.

The next two routes are across to the right, and take lines on the wall between the second and third ash trees.

PS 14 **Ringing Groove** 17m E1 5b *
The thin left-facing groove in the steep, clean wall. Exit left at its end to easier ground.

PS 15 **Sunspot** 17m E1 5b *
An excellent route and, like the last one, a tough proposition. Climb the groove which is just about behind the third ash, to a small roof. Pull out right into a flake crack, and then back left to good holds in a short wall.

Stoney Bank Crags

Low Stoney Bank GR SD 914644

Situation and access
This, the first crag of the pair, lies a few minutes' walk up the little valley above the waterfalls in Gordale Scar. From Malham village,

follow the right fork at the small grassed island and park at the end
of this road as for Gordale Scar. Walk up into the gorge, scramble
up the well-worn path alongside the waterfalls, up some steps and
drop down on to a path by the beckside. The crag is on the right
bank as one walks upstream.

Character
A steep crag, but not in the same league of intimidation as some of
its close neighbours. The valley is rather enclosed here and the crag
can remain damp and cold in the winter months, in which case a
visit to the higher crag is likely to be a better bet.

The climbs
These are described from left to right.

LSB 1   **KD**   45m   HVS   5a   5a   4c   *
    1. 9m 5a. Ascend the corner to a small ledge.
    2. 21m 5a. The wall on the left to a peg runner. Traverse
    right under a bulge and cross a smooth slab to a niche.
    3. 15m 4c. Climb the crack and avoid the roof by a traverse
    left to easier ground.

LSB 2   **Vanishing Point**   55m   E1   5c   5a   5b   **
    A good route which, as described, uses the second pitch of
    Happy Wanderer and the Tumeric Variation of that route as
    a third pitch.
    1. 25m 5c. Gain a break beneath the roof via a start just
    right of the last route. Traverse right with a crux just before
    the niche stance of Happy Wanderer.
    2. 10m 5a. Continue traversing the break to a yew tree.
    3. 20m 5b. Get into the hanging groove on the left and
    ascend the flake crack in the wall above.

LSB 3   **Pigs on the Wing**   30m   E3   6a   *
    8m right of KD is a round pocket at about 3m. Climb past
    this to the bottom of a slim left-slanting crack. Get to the

LSB (1–4)

roof by climbing a vague line on the left. Traverse 2m right
and pull boldly through the roof at its widest point. Easier
climbing up a rib to finish. Not bad.

LSB 4 **Happy Wanderer** 45m HVS 4a 5a 5b
1. 12m 4a. Start where three holes form a down-pointing
triangle (best viewed from a little way back from the foot of
the crag). From the base of this make a rising traverse right
to a niche under the roof.
2. 12m 5a. Reach the break and traverse right to a yew tree.
3. 20m 5b. As for pitch 3 of Vanishing Point (Tumeric
Variation).

High Stoney Bank   GR SD 912662

Situation and access
Approach as for Low Stoney Bank, but continue up the beckside
past that crag for a few minutes to reach a more pleasant-looking
crag on the same side of the beck.

Character
A more open crag with some good, if mostly short, routes on rock
which is usually excellent. This is a really smashing place to climb –
close to but away from the bulk of the crowds which so often
frequent Gordale, and attracting some afternoon sun even in winter.

The climbs
These are described from left to right.

HS 1 **Barbed Envy** 8m HS

HS 2 **Randy Mandy** 8m HVS 5a

LSB(1–4), Stoney Bank Crags, Low Stoney Bank

HS (1–27)

HS 3 **Unnatural Practice**   9m   VS   4c

HS 4 **Debauchery**   14m   VS   4c   *
Takes the shattered flake crack directly to finish just left of
the ash.

HS 5 **Latrina Direct Finish**   18m   VS   4c

HS 6 **Latrina**   22m   HS

HS 7 **Post Point-five Blues**   18m   HVS   5b
An indefinite crack in the centre of the wall. Quite strenuous.

HS 8 **Whet**   18m   HVS   5b

HS 9 **Dyre**   18m   HS
The shallow chimney, exiting leftwards at the top and
trending right to finish.

HS 10 **Cavity Wall**   18m   E3   5c

HS 11 **Depravity**   18m   HS   *
A handsome crack in the right-facing corner. Nice climbing
on sound rock.

HS 12 **Incest**   17m   VS   4c   *
Just round the arete is a short crack. Up this and left to a
ledge on the rib. Continue up the wall to easier ground.

HS 13 **Necrophilia**   18m   HVS   5a   *
The jam crack just right again, then the wall, bearing left to
a good hold on the rib.

HS(1–27), Stoney Bank Crags, High Stoney Bank

HS 14   **Squirm Crack**   17m   VS   4c
The wide corner crack can be climbed without squirming and is not quite as nasty as it looks.

HS 15   **The Deviate**   23m   VS   4c

There is now a steep and smooth wall, undercut at its base with two old aid lines.

HS 16   **Jocasta**   20m   ES   6b   *
A line of small pockets leads to a niche. Follow a line above this past two pegs to some flakes which lead, thankfully, to a rest.

HS 17   **Oedipus**   18m   E2   5c   **
A sustained route taking the right-hand line. Hard moves to a peg at 4m. Move right to a ledge and a series of short cracks. Continue without much respite up and leftwards to a bulge, after which the standard eases. A direct start is E2 6b.

HS 18   **Divers Groove Direct Start**   19m   HVS   5a   *
Strenuously up the overhanging groove to where it becomes a flake. Traverse right for 3m and follow the big groove to finish.

HS 19   **Divers Groove**   18m   MVS   4b

HS 20   **Sorotchinsky Fair**   18m   E3   6b
Climb on to the top of the large pedestal. Somewhat harder climbing to a small ledge and a direct finish.

HS 21   **Sodom Direct Start**   21m   HVS   5a
A crack cuts through two roofs, the upper one being smaller. Follow this and move right into a left-slanting groove which leads to some yews. Move left and climb a short wall to the top.

HS 22 **Sodom** 22m MVS

HS 23 **Gomorrah** 18m VS 4c *
A neat crack and groove line above the large free-standing flake.

HS 24 **Hors d'Oeuvres** 18m E2 5c

HS 25 **Ummagumma** 18m VS
Start 6m right of the flake and layback the crack round the roof to a poorer finish.

HS 26 **Lust** 18m VS 4c *
Aim for a large shallow cave 10m up. From this finish boldly up the steep chimney.

HS 27 **Come On, Come On** 20m E3 5c
Start at a shallow groove just right of two holes low down in the rock. Climb this groove and another up to the left. Up to the roof and boldly go for the right-slanting crack.

Twistleton Scars GR SD 716763

Situation and access
A high-level and exposed escarpment which faces south-west. It lies about 10 minutes' walk above a minor road which is reached as follows from the A65. From Ingleton, follow the B6255 towards Thornton in Lonsdale, which leads down towards some viaducts. After a short way, a minor road turns off to the right, signposted Beezley Farm. Follow this road up the hill and past the farm on to a more level road with a number of scars visible up to the left. Twistleton House Farm lies under the crag and parking is available here. Please always ask permission to park and climb, as there is no right of way to the crags from here. A small charge may be made for parking.

T (1–4)

Character
This is a wonderful place to climb, with a good selection of routes on
excellent rock and with a fine outlook. Its high and exposed position
makes it vulnerable to winds, but conversely, it dries quickly and
gets plenty of sunshine. An excellent afternoon and evening crag
with some classic routes in the easier grades.

The climbs
These are described from left to right, starting at Candle Buttress
which is on the left-hand side of the main crag above the farm.

T 1 **Candle Crack**   10m   VS   5a   *
   A difficult crack on the left of The Candle.

T 2 **The Candle**   11m   HVS   5b   ***
   A great climb which ascends the front of the buttress. Thin
   flake holds lead to the right edge of the small roof. Move left
   and finish direct in a fine position.

   40m right is a good-looking buttress containing some striking
   cracks.

T 3 **Clinker**   9m   D

T 4 **Wildwood**   9m   E1   5c

T 5 **Left-hand Crack**   9m   VD   *

T 6 **Right-hand Crack**   9m   S   *

T 7 **Handjam Crack**   8m   S   *
   This good crack lies just round the right side of the buttress.

T(1–4), Twistleton Scars

T (4-16)

20m right a large mushroom-shaped lump lies in front of the crag.

T 8 **Christine** 8m   D
The right chimney formed by the mushroom to its top and the wall behind.

T 9 **Skeleton Scoop** 8m   VD

T 10 **Serenity** 8m   VS

T 11 **Jimmy Jump** 9m   E1   5c
Aim for a thin crack right of Serenity and climb it strenuously.

The next part of the crag has a well-undercut base.

T 12 **Pericles** 10m   HS

T 13 **Winkle** 10m   HVS   5c
A difficult start typical of this section of the crag leads to thin cracks.

T 14 **Big Sur** 10m   E1   5c

T 15 **Rhubarb Crack** 10m   E1   5c   *
Another difficult pull gains the right-hand crack and easier but still interesting climbing.

T 16 **Bay Wall** 8m   D
The wall in the back of the bay gives a reasonable route. The chimney to the right is useful for descent.

T(4–16), Twistleton Scars

T (17–31)

T 17 **Curving Crack**   15m   VS   4c   ***
A real gem, giving athletic climbing on good holds, the first
section being the hardest. It lies up the front of the buttress
just right of the bay.

T 18 **Thornton Wall**   10m   VS   5a   **
Start below a crack which fails to reach the ground. A bold
series of moves brings good holds within reach. Finish to the
left.

T 19 **Twistleton Crack**   10m   VS   4c

T 20 **Twilight Wall**   12m   S

T 21 **Gorgo**   12m   VS   4c   *
The steady right-hand groove line is climbed, using the left
wall at times.

Moving right again is The Great Barrier, a steep wall with
an undercut base.

T 22 **Reefer**   16m   E4   6b   *
A vague line through the bulge 4m right of the left end of the
wall leads to a crack and relief. Sustained technical climbing
on small holds.

T 23 **Heavy Breather**   16m   E3   6a   **
Start just left of the right edge of The Barrier and aim for a
crack system. The overhang presents the main difficulty.

T 24 **Evening Star**   18m   S   **
An attractive corner right of The Barrier. The upper part is
reached via a slim lower corner and a leftwards traverse on
flakes. Very worthwhile.

T(17–31), Twistleton Scars

T, Twistleton Scars,
Priority

T 25 **Sickle Arete**   18m   VS   4c   *

T 26 **Sickle**   22m   VS   4c

T 27 **Sickle Direct**   18m   VS   5a   **
A really excellent route up the prominent corner.

T 28 **Priority Corner**   18m   S

T 29 **Priority**   20m   HS   4b   ***
Start just right of the corner and gain the rightwards-leading
flake. Follow this and climb the ensuing corner. Thoroughly
enjoyable.

T, Twistleton Scars,
Evening Star

T 30 **Superiority** 18m VS 5a *
A direct up the wall above Priority's flake.

T 31 **Priority Direct** 18m VS 4c
Gain Priority's final corner direct.

Beyond here are many short routes, often in the easier grades.

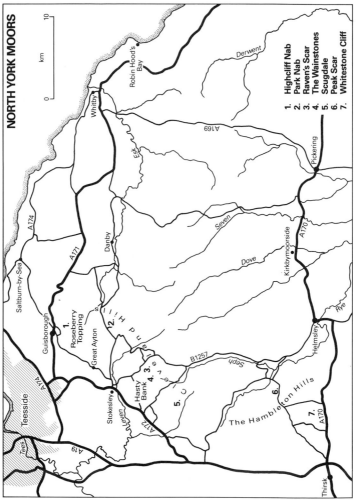

NORTH YORK MOORS

1. Highcliff Nab
2. Park Nab
3. Raven's Scar
4. The Wainstones
5. Scugdale
6. Peak Scar
7. Whitestone Cliff

North York Moors

North York Moors

Above the plains of North Yorkshire and the mammoth industrial complexes of flat Teesside rises an upland area of quiet beauty. On the edges and in the dells there are crags with much to offer the rock climber. Some areas are open while others nestle amongst the trees, and although the largest of the crags reach 30m generally they are much shorter than this.

The climbing rocks of the North York Moors consist of two main types – sandstone and limestone. However, both bear little resemblance to rocks elsewhere and the nature of the limestone in particular makes it an extremely demanding rock on which to climb. While caution should be exercised with the limestone at all times, the sandstone is generally more reliable with frequent intrusions of ironstone providing a useful source of holds.

There is much to go at and the climbing is uniquely rewarding whether it be the sunny non-serious bouldering on the fine little rocks of Scugdale or the ultimately gripping cemented sand and block limestone of the large Whitestone Cliff. Access is invariably quick and easy, if a little muddy on occasions, yet the moors retain an air of wildness often associated with much higher mountain areas. This is an interesting climbing area offering more than its small scale would at first suggest.

Highcliff Nab   GR NZ 610138

Situation and access
High above Guisborough the crag is quite accessible. If the Great Ayton to Guisborough road is followed, a road off to the right leads to Hutton Low Cross. Take a road to the right marked 'Cul-de-sac' until the metalled road ends and the Forestry begins. A gate here is usually left open and the track is followed up, bearing left at every junction, until a further gate, locked, just below the crag. From this

HN (1–7)

gate take the rising track until a path breaks steeply through the
wood to the left to emerge at the crag (30 minutes from the bottom
gate).

Character
Can be rather dank but some of the climbs are good.

The climbs
Ignore the graffiti-covered wall to the right. The routes are
described from right to left.

HN 1 **Highcliff Chimney Ordinary**   15m   VD

HN 2 **Highcliff Chimney Direct**   12m   S

HN 3 **Heart Throb Crack**   17m   HS   4b

HN 4 **Flake Crack**   17m   HVS   4c   *

   To the left is a wall with a distinctive ledge at about 5m.
   Two routes – Barnaby's Routes D – gain the ledge.

HN 5 **Highcliff Crack**   18m   S   **
   The crack leads to the top.

HN 6 **Queer Street**   21m   HVS   5a

HN 7 **Moonflower**   21m   E3   6a   *

HN 8 **Scarecrow Crack**   20m   HVS   5a   *
   The awkward and strenuous crack.

HN 9 **Stargazer**   17m   E3   5c

HN(1–7), Highcliff Nab

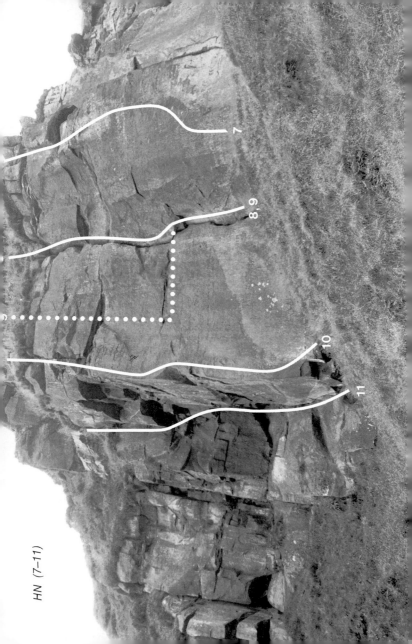

HN (7–11)

HN 10 **Magic in the Air**   17m   E5   6b   *

HN 11 **Wombat**   18m   HVS   5a   **
> An astonishing route. Climb the corner with some unique climbing.

Park Nab   GR NZ 608086

Situation and access
The crag is attractively situated on the hill above Park Farm in Kildale (south of Kildale village) just above the tiny Kildale to Baysdale road. Kildale is reached from Great Ayton or Stokesley and then the Baysdale road is briefly followed until a gate across the road gives access to the open moor. Either park just after the gate and walk steeply up to the crag or continue up the road to park in a little quarry on the left and then contour across to the crag (5 minutes).

Character
Small and compact but in many ways one of the most pleasant sandstone crags in the North York Moors. Generally facing west, with quick access, it is a good afternoon or evening climbing ground. Because it is so small, little description is necessary for the climbs but, even so, it is a crag and not just a boulder: most people rope up to tackle the climbs here.

The climbs
The routes are described from right to left.

PN 1 **The Bitter End**   6m   HVS   5b
> There is a letter-box hold – take a direct line using it.

HN(7–11), Highcliff Nab

PN (1–23)

PN(1–23), Park Nab

PN 2 **The Bowstring** 6m VS 5a

PN 3 **Long Bow** 6m HS *
The obvious crack.

PN 4 **Hara-kiri** 8m HVS 5a *

PN 5 **Pessimist** 6m E3 6a

PN 6 **Scoop Chimney** 6m VD

PN 7 **Wallbar Buttress** 6m VD

PN 8 **Chockstone Chimney** 6m D

PN 9 **Chairman's Climb** 8m VS 4b *

PN 10 **Pinnacle Crack – Right-hand** 6m VD

PN 11 **Pinnacle Crack – Left-hand** 6m D

PN 12 **Right Crack** 6m S

PN 13 **Left Crack** 6m D

PN 14 **Twin Cracks** 6m S

PN 15 **Twisting Chimney** 8m D

PN 16 **Styx** 8m E1 5c *

PN 17 **Shere Khan**   9m   E3   6a

PN 18 **Grumble and Grunt**   9m   HVS   5b   *
Getting stuck is a real hazard!

PN 19 **Castle Climb**   10m   VD

PN 20 **Cook's Gully, Table Climb**   8m   M

PN 21 **Cook's Gully, Left Chimney**   9m   D

PN 22 **Zero Route**   5m   HVS   5a

PN 23 **Lion's Jaw**   6m   HVS   5b

Peak Scar   GR SE 527884

Situation and access
The crag lies just below the Hawnby to Boltby road in a ravine
bedecked with many trees. On the steep hill from Hawnby the crag
can be found after the road levels off, and a small gate through the
fence on the north (right) side of the road leads down into the wood.
The path veers left into the ravine and continues beneath the rocks
(5 minutes).

Character
In many respects this is one of the best crags in the North York
Moors. Despite its northerly aspect, situated in a wooded ravine, it
is sheltered and often in condition. The crag is extensive, reaching a
height of 27m and the distinct lines give very good climbing. The
rock is of the same geological type of limestone as Whitestone Cliff
but is sounder; while this gives the climbing a unique flavour great
caution must be exercised for holds and blocks do break off.

The climbs
The routes are described from left to right. The first, rather scruffy,
wall ends in a prow with a distinct corner crack to its right. Right of
this, above the now level path, is the first wall to be described here.
The first climb described takes a hanging crack left of the distinct
corner.

PK 1 **Dat Der**   20m   VS   4c   **
    A strenuous climb with a particularly absorbing lower
    section. Care should be taken on the top ledge which is often
    muddy.

PK 2 **Jordu**   23m   VD   **
    Steep, but the holds are good.

PK 3 **Fifi**   23m   HVS   5b
    The wall 2m right of Jordu is climbed direct – left of the
    obvious top block overhang. The wall leads to a ledge and
    then a corner leads to the overhang. Pull over this to
    continue up the cracks above.

PK 4 **Pianississimo**   23m   VS   4c   ***
    Climb directly up the wall, with interest, to the large block
    jammed in the overhang (The Battleship). Pull through the
    roof (with more than a little trepidation) using this and
    continue by a wall and chimney to the top.

PK 5 **Ackers**   24m   VS   4c

PK 6 **Ornithology**   27m   S   *
    Climb the flakes and move left to the tree. Use this to climb
    the overhang and up to continue horizontally left along the
    break. Finish up the chimney of Pianississimo.

PK 7 **Pemba Chimney**   24m   D
    The block chimney.

PK(1–7), Peak Scar, Pianississimo Wall

Pemba Chimney marks the end of this wall. Right of this is
the Main Wall but it is rather overgrown to begin with and
the next climbs described are some 20 yards to the right.
There is a large ash tree at two-thirds height, and just right
of this and a little lower a smaller ash (this is seen on the
photograph). A further point of identification is the fact that
the next two climbs also start from a narrowing platform, as
the Main Wall tumbles away below to the right.

PK 8 **Wings** 27m S *

Climb directly by a series of small ledges to the small ash. Move left and climb through the overhang using the crack to a recess below the final corner – it is usual to finish left of this.

PK 9 **Birdland Direct** 27m MVS 4b **

Climb 3m right of Wings to find an awkward crack leading to a ledge below the distinct corner. This leads directly

upwards to the left of the impressive prow at the top of the crag. The corner is gained and the crack followed to the top.

To the right from the lowest point of a hollow a distinct jagged crack splits the wall.

PK 10 **Jam with Sam**   27m   VS   4b   **
Gain the crack and follow it to the top. A popular route – it must be the name!

The Main Wall continues until (to the right of a particularly vegetated bottom section) there is an obvious groove which is the line of the next climb.

PK 11 **Gone**   27m   HS   *
The groove and wall to surmount the overhang and continue directly to the top.

PK 12 **Milestones**   27m   VS   4c
Rather a serious feel for the grade. Climb the glaring detached flake on its edge – a tree grows in the rift. Climb through the overhang via a break and ascend the wall above to a narrow ledge. Traverse left to a block and up to a wide crack which is climbed to a finish on the right.

PK 13 **Frenesi**   27m   VS   4c   **
Step off the block and climb the steep wall to a narrow ledge. Move over the overhang (there are good holds) and up the wall moving leftwards to a ledge. Move out from the right end of the ledge pulling up the bulge (crux) to gain a crack in the wall. Finish directly to the top. A big route.

PK 14 **Downbeat**   21m   VD
The corner chimney.

PK(8–10), Peak Scar, left-hand Main Wall

PK (11–15)

1

12

PK(11–15), Peak Scar, right-hand Main Wall

Murton Cave

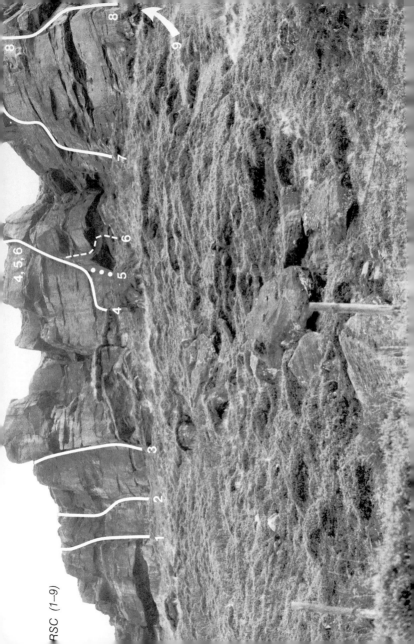

RSC (1-9)

PK 15 **Walking**   21m   HVD

> To the right of this route is a sharp edge marking the end of
> the Main Wall and right of this again a deep dark corner
> cleft of some interest – Murton Cave (M). This is most often
> used in descent but an ascent reconnoitre is recommended
> beforehand. There are climbs to the right again but they are
> not described here.

Raven's Scar   GR NX 566037

Situation and access
This crag is on the north flank of Hasty Bank and overlooks the
Vale of Cleveland. Beyond Great Broughton on the Stokesley to
Helmsley road there is a large car-park near the summit of Clay
Bank. Leading into the wood, just above this, is a path which soon
reaches a track. The track rises steeply and then contours along the
flank of Hasty Bank. The first quarry-like walls up on the left are *not*
Raven's Scar. Continue along past these until a larger, even blacker,
crag appears (20 minutes).

Character
Despite Raven's Scar's lichenous, cold and forbidding appearance,
there are some worthwhile climbs – and by North York Moors'
standards the crag is a large one.

The climbs
The routes are described from left to right.

RSC 1 **En Passant**   11m   S

RSC 2 **Lazy Bones**   11m   MVS   4a

RSC(1–9), Raven's Scar

RSC 3 **Satchmo** 14m E1 5b **
A strenuous start gives access to a good climb.

RSC 4 **Ahab** 12m HS 4b *
The hand traverse leads right to the corner. The corner leads
to a ledge and then a crack to a perched block.

RSC 5 **Ahab Direct Start** 12m E1 5c
The groove direct.

RSC 6 **Jonah** 12m HVS 5a *
Climb through the roof to enter the groove. Join Ahab and
follow this to the top.

RSC 7 **Forest Face** 20m MVS 4b
Move up leftwards to a ledge and then traverse right to a
small groove. Up this with difficulty and move right to a
crack. The crack and chimney lead to the top.

RSC 8 **Harlot's Groove** 17m VS 4c *
Gain the roof and move left into a groove. Continue in a
direct line to the top.

RSC 9 **Tumble Down Dick** 26m D
The chimney to a ledge and then the rocks on the left to
finish up a corner.

Scugdale GR NZ 520004

Situation and access
Facing pretty much south, 'sunny Scuggy' is a sheltered climbing
ground despite its 300m altitude. Swainby lies off the A172 (just
before it joins the A19 Middlesbrough to Thirsk road). Drive
through the village (either side of the stream at first); shortly beyond

SCUG(A), Scugdale

it a road marked 'Cul-de-sac' leads over a ford to the left. Drive up this for 4 miles until a parking space (limited) and stile on the left are reached. From here one can see the line of crags on the hillside – a well-defined path leads directly to the right-hand end (4 minutes).

Character
The premier bouldering area of the North York Moors and well worth a visit. Most of the routes are around 6m high but for a few a rope will be thought necessary. The sandstone is superb and whilst many of the walls are off-vertical there are routes of all standards – almost 200 routes have been recorded – with sufficient climbing to entertain all. A long afternoon can be enjoyed here both by those seeking technical and strenuous bouldering and by those wanting a more moderate day's climbing.

SCUG(B), Scugdale, Drunken Buttress

The climbs

Individual description of the routes is unnecessary – the standard of difficulty is usually self-evident. To the right of the point of arrival is a fence and the climbs stretch leftwards from here, up to and including the last visible buttress.

The Wainstones   GR NZ 559036

Situation and access

This crag is on the western end of Hasty Bank and its distinctive
needles are clearly seen in profile from Broughton and the Vale of
Cleveland way below. Beyond Great Broughton on the Stokesley to
Helmsley road there is a large car-park near the summit of Clay
Bank. Leading into the wood, just above this, is a path which
shortly reaches a track. The track rises steeply and then contours
horizontally along the flank of Hasty Bank. Continue along the track
(beneath Raven's Scar) until near the end of the bank a path leads
up left to the rocks (30 minutes).

Character

The pinnacles of the Wainstones are readily identified from some
distance and consequently this is one of the oldest climbing grounds
in the North York Moors. The sandstone contains a number of
ironstone inclusions and these form useful holds on several routes.
The main Bilsdale Face looks west and remains a popular place to
climb. Despite the fact that all the climbs are short, the routes offer
surprising variety and character, and the rock is sound and clean.

The climbs

The Bilsdale Face is to the right of the approach ridge. The routes
are described from left to right. The Needle is the lower pinnacle
and the Steeple the upper; both can be climbed by various routes,
the easiest being about Difficult in standard.

WST 1 **Little Bo-Peep**   11m   HS   4b
From the block in the gully hand traverse left for 2.5m until
a pull on to a ledge ends the difficulties.

WST 2 **Ling Buttress**   9m   HS   4a   *
A triangular recess marks the route.

WST(1–9), The Wainstones

WST 3 **West Sphinx Climb** 11m HVS 5b **
From the right ascend diagonally left to move out from
beneath the overhang on to the wall above. Move up to a
pocket and step right to continue to the top.

WST 4 **East Sphinx Climb** 9m HVS 5a
The slight crack and the wall direct.

WST 5 **Sphinx Nose Traverse** 11m S *
Start in the corner and move up and left to a crack. Traverse

the break to the left to gain the front edge of the buttress and
ascend to the top.

WST 6 **Bulge Superdirect**   9m   HVS   5c
The start provides an interesting problem.

WST 7 **The Bulge**   11m/35ft   HS   4a
From the foot of the gully move up and then spiral left until
the climbing eases to the top.

WST 8 **Wall and Ledge**   11m   D

WST 9 **Ali Baba**   9m   E1   5b   *

Whitestone Cliff   GR SE 507836

Situation and access
This large crag, just north of Sutton Bank above Thirsk, faces west
and commands a fine position over the patchwork of agricultural
plains below. Access is from the large car-park (and visitors' centre)
at the top of Sutton Bank, on the A170 from Thirsk. Proceed north
along the path (marked 'Cleveland Way') that skirts the top edge of
the bank. After about a mile the bushes and trees to the left of the
path disappear – slightly beyond the northern shore of Gormire
Lake down in the hollow below – and this signals the start of the cliff
(15 minutes). A gully leads down to the bottom of the cliff from this
point. The wall described here lies just around a distinguished
stepped overhanging arete to the right (facing down the gully). The
gully starts with grass but rapidly steepens and transforms into
polished clay! Care must be taken even in the driest conditions but if
the descent is at all wet it is wisest to fix a safety rope or abseil.
There is a small bush just as the grass turns to clay but it may be
better to fix something further back – nearer the top.

Character
This cliff is large and extensive but due to the nature of the rock the
only recommended climbing is on the wall described here. On this
steep clean wall the rock is at its best and the climbing, following the
distinct vertical cracks, enjoyable. However, care should be
exercised at all times because holds do break off! The rock is unique,
apparently some kind of oolitic limestone, but it is best described as
a mixture of sand and pebbles weakly cemented together – the
cement being strongest in the area described!

The climbs
The routes are described from right to left. Immediately left of the
arete, forming the obvious and impressive corner crack, is the first
route.

WST(4), East Sphinx Climb, The Wainstones

WS (1–3)

WS 1 **Nightwatch**   34m   HS   4b   ***
The frequent horizontal cracks make this climb less fearsome
than first appearances would suggest. Nevertheless,
difficulties are sustained until the top. Use a tree well back
from the edge to belay. The grade given is traditional and
many who are unfamiliar with the rock may find it harder.

WS 2 **Central Crack**   34m   HVS   5a   **
The crack is followed throughout. Particular care must be
taken with any block holds and it is recommended that
regular protection is sought.

WS 3 **Countdown Direct**   34m   HVS   5a   *
The crack through the bulge to the ledge. Step left and
continue up the crack to the top.

WS(1–3), Whitestone Cliff

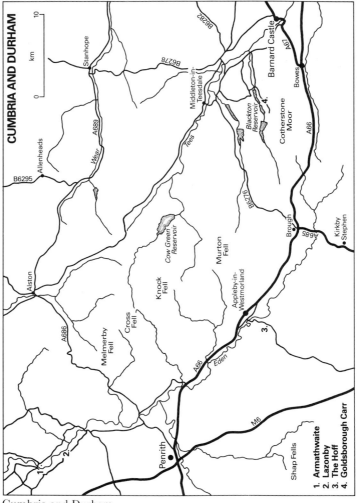

CUMBRIA AND DURHAM

1. **Armathwaite**
2. **Lazonby**
3. **The Hoff**
4. **Goldsborough Carr**

Cumbria and Durham

Cumbria and Durham

This is the area sandwiched between the North York Moors to the south and Northumberland to the north. While the sandstone crags of Cumbria, in the Eden valley, are particularly significant for those based in Carlisle or the Lake District, providing a useful alternative in poor weather, they are also worth a visit in their own right and their proximity to the M6 should not be forgotten. The Hoff, located near the old Westmorland county town of Appleby, is also included for, although small, it offers unique climbing on a conglomerate rock. The crags of Durham are more scattered within the region and only Goldsborough Carr, close to Barnard Castle, was thought to be of sufficient quality to be included here.

The Eden Valley

Armathwaite   GR NY 505452

Situation and access
These crags are in a delightful setting on the east bank of the River Eden. The sun comes fully on to them in the afternoon and they are often at least partly in a climbable condition even in poor weather. The village of Armathwaite is easily reached from the A6 Carlisle to Penrith road by a turning at Mason's Garage. Park at the bridge over the river and use the obvious stile to gain access to the riverside path which is followed upstream for about 15 minutes to the crag, keeping left where the path splits.

Character
The rock is sandstone of variable quality. At best it provides excellent climbing and at worst it gives some snappy routes which should be avoided. The worst areas of rock tend to be red and the

AR (1–4)

looseness is obvious. Visitors should remember that many of the routes here are top-roped as the norm by many climbers and that some of the leads are quite serious. On a sunny evening, the situation takes some beating.

The climbs
The first part of the crag reached is above a sandy bay. This is easily recognized by the permanent chalk marks and the overhanging nature of the rock. The routes are described from left to right.

AR 1 **Time and Motion Man**   17m   HVS   5a   **
> Starts at a recess below and right of an obvious groove. Some strenuous contortions lead to good holds and the groove. Leave this to the left to a ledge and climb worryingly out past a very spiny gorse bush. Leap well out to the left in the event of a fall to gain access to a soft but wet landing.

AR 2 **The Exorcist**   E4   5c   17m   **
> A short corner in the centre of the wall contains a piton. Climb up to this by one of a variety of options and use a rib on the right to move up with difficulty to good holds. Gain a ledge (or take some air) and continue the pump to the top via a groove. Sustained and strenuous.

AR 3 **Blast Off**   16m   E3   5c

AR 4 **Glenwillie Grooves**   13m   HS   4b   *
> The open groove on the right of the steep wall gives an interesting route with a thought-provoking finish.

Upstream from here, a couple of short buttresses are passed to reach the Main Buttress, a wall packed with features.

AR(1–4), Armathwaite, Exorcist area

AR 5 The Bullgine Run 32m   VD   **

Climb on to a ledge on the front of the main wall which has
a number of stout young oaks growing from it. The meat of
the route takes the attractive right slanting slab on good
holds and with exciting moves. Really good for its grade.

AR 6 Flasherman 27m   MVS   **

A great climb which starts round to the right of the main
wall beneath a good-looking corner. A short slab topped by a
roof is climbed and then quitted on good holds which lead
up towards the corner. Follow the corner to the top of the
flake, traverse right, move up, then go back left to finish.

AR 7 Erection 30m   VS   4c   ***

A classy and sustained route. Start at a short wall beneath
the large rock willy, just right of the start of the last route. A
tricky start leads to cracks and the underside of the willy.
Entertaining moves around the end of it lead to a short final
wall which is poorly protected but well supplied with the
necessary.

Domed Slab

This buttress lies just across to the right from the last routes
and has a conspicuous overhang on its upper right-hand
side.

AR 8 Close Encounters 8m   HVS   5b

AR 9 Dome Slab 15m   E3   5c   *

Climb a steep wall below the right side of the big roof for
6m. Move right and utilize some pockets to reach a
horizontal crack. Follow the line out through the roof to a
hard finish.

AR(5–9), Armathwaite, Erection area

AR(10–11), Armathwaite, Red Buttress

Red Buttress

Poor rock on its left side, but better on the slabs on the right.

AR 10 **Wafer Thin** 11m E5 6a/b
A desperate problem which sees very few leads. The rib is followed via thin flakes and a variety of poor holds to a horrendous pull on to the slab.

AR 11 **Paper Moon** 12m E1 5b **
Delightful climbing up the curving underlap leads to a puzzling move back left, using a vertical crack.

AR 12 **Free and Easy** 11m E2 5c **

An excellent route on a buttress across to the right, and
recognizable by a short curving crack at its top. Climb the
wall below this and pull through the bulge with difficulty to
another hard move on little pockets which gains the base of
the crack. This is slightly easier but still requires thought.

AR(12–15), Armathwaite, Sailing Shoes area

AR 13 **Sailing Shoes**   11m   E4   5c

AR 14 **The Crescent**   13m   HVS   5a   *
Climb the left slanting ramp from the jammed boulder until
a stretch gains a good hold. Pull up and wander up the slab
above.

AR 15 **Jelly Terror**   9m   HVS   5a
The broken crack line.

AR 16 **Barnacle Bill**   9m   HVS   5a   *
A popular climb up the appealing corner, with some
worrying moves near the top, which is often greasy.

AR 17 **Andy's Slab**   12m   E2   5c
The slab is climbed rightwards to a left slanting line where
things get easier. This route is often not in perfect condition,
when it can feel very hard.

AR 18 **Codpiece**   11m   E1   5b
The thin flared crack is climbed at this grade in perfect
conditions, but is harder when a little greasy.

AR 19 **Pickpocket Direct**   E1   5b

Lazonby   GR NY 527423

Situation and access
These east-facing crags lie on the bank of the River Eden, a few
miles upstream and on the opposite side from the Armathwaite
crags. From the main A6 Carlisle to Penrith road, turn left (when
southbound) at the Ministry of Agriculture AI Centre a couple of
miles north of Plumpton. Turn right after a mile or so and follow to

AR(16–19), Armathwaite, Codpiece area

a T junction with the Baronwood to Lazonby road. Turn right here,
cross a cattle grid and look for a track that leads down through fields
a few hundred yards further on. (This track can be recognized by
some large piles of stones a short way down it.) Park here, walk
down the track and across the railway. Bear right, passing a small
round copse of conifers, and follow a small path to the top of the
crags and a descent path on the right (facing the river).

Character
An exciting and serious place to climb with some good, long routes.
The rock is very variable sandstone, often good where it counts, but
with wafery flakes which tend to snap just when you thought they
were safe. Handle with care. On a sunny morning, a competent
team will enjoy a unique atmosphere.

The climbs
The first crag from the descent path is Cave Buttress, recognizable
by the cave up on its left. The rock here is not good.

Wirewalk Buttress

The obvious river-edge crag with the remains of the wire
handrail from which the name derives. The first route is
found on the Upstream Face, which faces the descent path.

LC 1 **Fingers**   29m   E1   5b   *
1. 15m 5b. Start at an attractive but now rather green wall
under a large birch. Fine but scary climbing gains the tree
and a stance.
2. 14m 5a. Climb the wall behind the tree via a crescent-
shaped overlap, moving right to finish in a fine position.

LC 2 **Silicosis**   31m   HVS   5a
Start at a recess where the Upstream Face becomes the

LC(1–5), Lazonby, Wirewalk Buttress

Riverside Face.
1. 15m 5a. A tricky wall and the ensuing flake-filled crack lead to a stance on the left.
2. 16m 4c. Traverse right and climb an exposed gangway to a finishing corner.

LC 3 **Gadzowt** 33m VS 4b
The easiest climb on the face starting at a steep crack which opens into a groove beneath a huge roof.
1. 15m 4b. Climb the grassy crack awkwardly which leads to an impressive situation beneath the roof. Traverse left to a ledge and belay.
2. 18m 4b. Ascend a blunt rib on the right, move right and top out via a short crack.

4m right of the start of Gadzowt is a fine-looking crack which unfortunately ends a couple of metres below the foot of the crag. The excellent Redchipper E3 5c gains this and follows it to the big ledges from where a variety of finishes are possible.

LC 4 **Merry Monk** 33m HVS 5a ***
An excellent route, marred only by the huge white piles – it must be a big bird! Start at a steep corner in the centre of the crag.
1. 15m 4b. The corner leads steeply but on good holds to a poor stance.
2. 16m 5a. Continue up the groove until a pretty wild move out right leads to a ledge. Belay, or continue rightwards up the short wall.

LC 5 **Cobweb** 31m E3 5b *
Start 5m right of Merry Monk at a weakness in the impending wall.
1. 15m 5b. Gain a right-facing groove via some steep and trying moves. Pull out right to the jamming crack and gain a

good ledge via a dubious block. Very poor belays, or carry
pegs, or if rope drag permits continue up the next pitch.
2. 16m 4c. Aim for a chimney-groove via a short wall and
exit right.

Goldsborough Carr   GR NY 954175

Situation and access
Within a short drive of Barnard Castle this crag, although fairly
high on Cotherstone Moor above the reservoirs in Balderdale, is
easily reached from the road below. Take the B6277 road from
Barnard Castle towards Middleton-in-Teesdale until just through
the village of Cotherstone a road, signposted 'East Briscoe', leads off
to the left. Continue along this road, passing the reservoir and then
through two gates to gain the open moor. Goldsborough Carr is the
distinct table-top hill immediately to the left. Keep up the road a
little way until a vague track leads up left to the rocks (5 minutes).
There is ample parking space.

Character
A delightful crag of perfect fine-grained grit, ideal for a short day or
evening. The rocks form the rim of the table-top and consist of a
north face overlooking the road and a south face at the back of the
hill.

The climbs
First the north and then the south faces are described from left to
right.

The North Face

GB 1 **Flakeaway**   5m   VD
Take the flake crack and finish up a short crack right of the
overhanging block at the top.

GB (1–10)

GB 2 **Scoon Arete**   3m   S   *

GB 3 **Bentley's Arete**   5m   HS   ***

GB 4 **Howgill Wall**   6m   VS   4c   *
Climb the bulging wall to the flake and up this to the impending ledge. Traverse left then move right through the overhang to finish.

GB 5 **Hagworm**   5m   VS   4b
The top of the prow is gained and then the overhanging rock just to the left of its top.

GB 6 **Friar Wall**   5m   HS

GB 7 **Tuck**   3m   D

GB 8 **Wriggle Up**   3m   HS   4b   *
The undercut slab from the left and finish left through the overhang.

GB 9 **Blockton Way**   3m   S   *

GB 10 **Block and Tackle**   3m   S

South Face

Buttress 1 Easily identified by the large flake leaning against the crag.

GB 11 **Y-crack**   3m   VD

GB 12 **Finger Crack**   3m   HS   4c

GB(1–10), Goldsborough Carr, North Face

GB (11–22)

GB 13 **Flake and Crack**   5m   S   *

GB 14 **Cenopod Corner**   3m   D

GB 15 **Hunder Crack**   5m   VD

Buttress 2

GB 16 **Yawd Sike**   5m   VS   4b
Ascend the centre of the wall direct.

Buttress 3

GB 17 **Fiddler on the Roof**   9m   E1   5b   ***
Climb the roof, using an interesting leg bar, to reach holds
above the lip. Continue directly up the wall to finish.

GB 18 **Unknown**   9m   E2   5c   **
A few metres right another weakness is discernible through
the roof. Use the flake to take an undercut pinch hold. A
long reach up right to the bottom of a ramp gives a good
hold. Follow the flake ramp diagonally leftwards and then
straight up the centre of the wall. Protection is scarce and
care should be taken with lichen in the top half.

Buttress 5

GB 19 **Fiddler Arete**   6m   HVS   5b   ***
Starting the arete is the hardest bit; the climbing above
excellent.

GB 20 **Fiddler**   6m   E1   5b   **
Gain a position on the undercut wall; then directly to the top.

GB(11–22), Goldsborough Carr, South Face

Diagonal Crack Buttress The last block on the right end of the south face.

GB 21 **Diagonal Crack**   5m   VD
The obvious left to right weakness.

GB 22 **Diagonal Direct**   3m   S
The wall directly up its centre.

The Hoff   GR NY 677180

Situation and access
A short outcrop of conglomerate Brockram – a mixture of limestone and sandstone – which gives lovely climbing and bouldering in a pastoral setting and is ideal after wet weather or for a short visit. Access is from the B6260 Appleby to Orton road. The crag can be seen on the north side of the road near Hoff, and there is room near here for roadside parking. There is no right of way to the crag, so ensure that no litter is left, and as the field frequently houses a dairy herd, dogs are better left in the car.

Character
Despite the climb's brevity it is still full of character and worth a short visit. Indeed, it is a useful venue for those passing nearby with little time to spare. But beware, the charms of The Hoff have over-extended many a lunch break.

The climbs

H 1 **The Shades**   4b

H 2 **Mojo**   4a

GB(19), Fiddler Arete, Goldsborough Carr

H (1–7)

H(1–7), The Hoff (left)

H, The Hoff, Barwise (right)

H 3 **Gromerzog**   5a/b   *

H 4 **Blonde Ella**   4b

H 5 **Barwise**   4b   *

H 6 **Wormrigg Wall**   4a

H 7 **Burrells**   4a

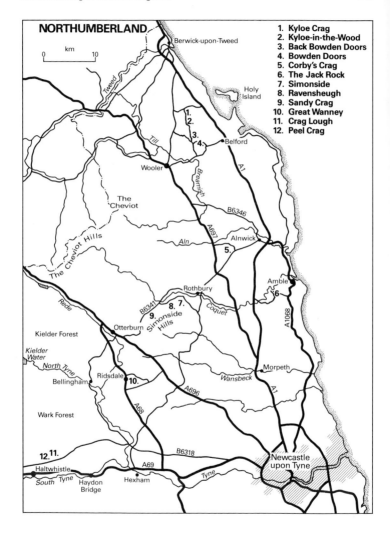

NORTHUMBERLAND

km
0   10

Berwick-upon-Tweed

Tweed

Holy
Island

1.
2.

3.
4.   Belford

Till

Wooler

Breamish

The
Cheviot

B6346

The Cheviot Hills

Aln   A697   Alnwick

5.

Rede

Rothbury   Amble

B6341   8. 7.   6.

9.   Coquet

Otterburn Simonside
Hills

Kielder Forest   A1068

Kielder
Water

North Tyne

Bellingham Ridsdale 10.   Morpeth

Wansbeck   A1

Wark Forest   A696

A68

12. 11.   B6318   Newcastle
upon Tyne

Haltwhistle   A69

South Tyne Haydon   Hexham   Tyne
Bridge

1. Kyloe Crag
2. Kyloe-in-the-Wood
3. Back Bowden Doors
4. Bowden Doors
5. Corby's Crag
6. The Jack Rock
7. Simonside
8. Ravensheugh
9. Sandy Crag
10. Great Wanney
11. Crag Lough
12. Peel Crag

Northumberland

This splendidly quiet county, located on the east coast between the industrial North-east and the Scottish border, offers a variety of climbing on crags mostly composed of the best sandstone in England. It is a great rolling county of much space and little population, a mixture of fertile plains and purple heather-covered moors, with most of the exposed rock occurring where the plains rise and fold upwards.

There are crags here to suit many tastes, from those by the roadside to those perched high in a remote setting. The climbing is equally varied: although the maximum height achieved is only 30m, there is a huge selection of grades and types of climbing. The sandstone is fine-grained, offering excellent friction, and despite the propensity for jamming it tends to be much kinder on the hands than gritstone. It also runs to sharp edge holds, incuts and pockets. However, one thing that must be declared is that, whether the rock be Whin Sill or the more common sandstone, the climbing is invariably steep and strenuous.

Despite the northerly latitude, climbing in the county can be a year-round activity, if the crag is suitably selected. Indeed many northern raiding parties travel over the border to climb here when their higher crags are out of condition – the Kyloe Crags and the Bowden Doors group, for example, are just as near to Edinburgh as they are to Newcastle and they are noted for their sheltered, hospitable locations.

Back Bowden Doors (Colour Heugh)   GR NU 065336

Situation and access

This south-west facing crag, lesser brother of Bowden Doors, is marked as Dancing Green Hill on the map (OS L75). It lies in a sheltered position above a shallow valley, its northern half protected from the wind by a conifer plantation. Access is easy, a few minutes' walk. Follow the B6349 from Belford towards Wooler (as for Bowden Doors) until the road forks. Take the right fork (about 2½ miles along from Belford) and follow this to the top of the hill. There is a metal gate and restricted parking on the verge with views to the small rocks of Dancing Hill on the right. Back Bowden lies approximately 500 yards from here and is reached by taking the track after the gate to another gate and then down, into the little valley, to a small bridge and another gate. The first rocks, in two tiers, are found just up to the right, with the main section of crag along by the plantation a short distance ahead. Although access has traditionally been no problem a recent spate of selfish behaviour has put the situation under review. Therefore to preserve access remember there should be no fires, no bivouacking (hoffing) or building up of walls beneath the overhangs and absolutely no litter left in the area (any litter spotted should be picked up).

Character

Although this crag is slightly smaller (in length) than Bowden Doors it is noted for its large roof-like overhangs. Despite this the rock is excellent, with not only a number of formidably hard routes (some of the hardest in Northern England) but also a good selection of easier routes. There are routes to climb roped and many strenuous problems. The first buttress, split at mid-height by a large ledge, is reached in a few minutes after which the crag breaks up until a prominent sweeping arc, just before the edge of the conifer plantation, forms an eye-catching marker – this is the edge of The Tube wall and the start of the main climbing area.

BB(13), The Tube, Back Bowden Doors

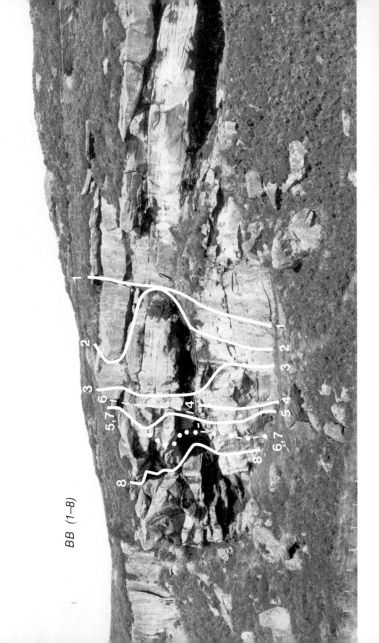

BB (1–8)

The climbs

The routes are described from right to left. The first route takes the right end of the first distinct buttress.

BB 1 **Final Wall**   12m   VD
The wall and then the easy corner crack.

BB 2 **Traverse Route**   15m   VD
Climb the ragged crack to the ledge and move right to the foot of the heather corner. Up to horizontal cracks which lead left on to the nose of the buttress. Continue until the top can be reached.

BB 3 **Original Route**   14m   VD   **
A good route up the highest section of this buttress. Climb the weakness and continue on good holds up the chimney to the ledge and a possible stance below the overhangs. Break through the overhangs at the weakest point right of Wall and Crack.

BB 4 **Pinup**   8m   E1   5b   *
Absorbing climbing finishing at the break.

BB 5 **Hazelrigg Wall**   14m   HVS   5a   *
Climb the wall and move left to finish left of the corner crack – where Roof Route comes in from the left.

BB 6 **Wall and Crack**   12m   S   4b
Follow the diagonal crack, then climb the corner crack above on the right (good holds).

BB 7 **Roof Route**   12m   E1   5b   *
The diagonal crack as for Wall and Crack then take the

BB(1–8), Back Bowden Doors, Two-Tier Buttress

BB (9-11)

overhanging crack through the roof above. Good holds at the top of the crack then move right to finish easily.

BB 8 **March Line** 11m   S
The crack to the ledge then traverse left to gain the nose (can be done directly) to find easier cracks leading to the top.

The crag now breaks up. The next route described starts right of the prominent sweeping prow of the smooth wall.

BB 9 **Gangway** 9m   VS   4c
The ramp right of the corner finishing up the slab or crack to the right.

BB 10 **Angle Corner** 9m   HVD
The right-angled corner. Climb to twin cracks and continue steeply to the top.

BB 11 **Duke of York** 12m   HVS   5a
Traverses the smooth wall from left to right. The flake crack reaches a ledge, gain the fault on the right and hand traverse until Angle Corner is reached.

BB 12 **Smith's Wall** E6   7a   10m

BB 13 **The Tube** 15m   E4   5c   ***
A fine sustained route offering excellent climbing up to, then along under, the wave overhanging the smooth wall. Climb the crack to a ledge then follow the rightward trending scoop to the roof. Protection can be arranged here and along the traverse but is strenuous to place. Traverse right for 6m until a weakness allows the bulge to be surmounted on to the slab above – good protection at this point.

BB(9–11), Back Bowden Doors, right side Tube Buttress

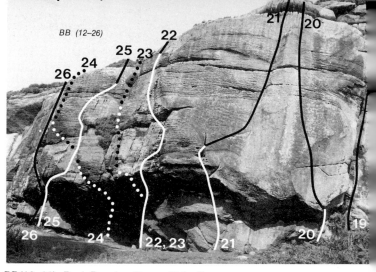

BB(12–26), Back Bowden Doors, Tube Buttress

BB 14 **Forester's Corner**   11m   D
Gain the midway ledges from the right and finish up the crack in the back.

BB 15 **Woodcutter's Crack**   11m   HVD
The left-hand crack to the recess and finish up the left-hand crack.

BB 16 **On the Verge**   11m   E4   6a
A thin crack is followed to pull out on to a ledge beneath the slab. Move up the edge of the slab making a hard series of moves until a crack provides an easy finish.

BB 17 **Magic Flute**   11m   E1   5b
From the corner make a move to gain the hanging ledge on the right. Move delicately up the slab to the flutings.

BB 18 **Golden Stairs**   12m   VD
The initial step is the hardest – start from the boulder on the right.

BB 19 **Straight Crack**   12m   MVS   4b

BB 20 **The Spell**   12m   E1   5c
A flake is used to gain the horizontal break and then the fluting is taken to the top.

The edge of the conifer plantation marks the start of the unique roof section of the crag. The 2.5m roof, situated at 2.5m height, provides a number of strenuously entertaining problems.

BB 21 **The Sorcerer**   14m   E1   5c   ***
The right-hand weakness of this notable roof. A very long reach enables holds in the lip and a pull gives a jam behind the fluting above. From here a transfer right is made to ascend the steep scoop directly to the top.

BB(26–32), Back Bowden Doors

BB 22 **Sorcerer's Apprentice** 14m E1 5b **
A prominent nose below the roof enables the lip to be
reached. Pull up into the central flake crack. Trend left to
follow easier rocks to the top.

BB 23 **The Vole** 14m E1 5c *
Once the lip is reached, and this is interesting enough, move
left to make a very technical/strenuous move using a flake
crack to pull on to the wall above. Step left and continue to
the top.

BB 24 **Black Magic** 14m 5c *
Gain the groove with some difficulty and continue until at its
top a traverse left leads to a blunt arete which is followed to
the top.

BB 25 **The Wizard** 14m HVS 5b *
Hand traverse to the slab and climb it to finish up the
groove.

BB 26 **Bottle Crack** 12m HS 4c

BB 27 **The Enchanter** 14m E2 5c
A scoop leads to the horizontal break and then directly up
the wall until a traverse right leads to flutings.

BB(33–39), Back Bowden Doors, left end

BB 28 **The Broomstick**   14m   E2   5b   **
The central weakness up the wall with a long reach at the top.

BB 29 **The Wand**   12m   E2   5b   *

BB 30 **The Witch**   15m   E2   5b   **
The fluting leads to the overhang. Make an ascending traverse right until the end of the overhang then finish straight up.

BB 31 **Holly Tree Corner**   12m   S   4b

36 35 34 33

BB 32 **The Arches**   15m   HVS   5a   ***
A tremendous route starting from the sandwiched slab on
the left and making an ascending traverse rightwards
between the roofs above and overhangs below. The finish
breaks out directly up the wall and is blessed by good holds.

The next section of crag leftwards comes in the form of a
constantly overhanging black wall – it is breached by three
(Bob Smith) routes at an average grade of 6c. Some high
threads indicate the way should you wish to follow them.

BB 33 **Twisting Crack**   8m   MVS   4c

BB 34 **Broken Glass**   11m   E1   5b

BB 35 **Glass Slipper** 12m   VS   5a
The slab to the overlap with a good foothold before
launching up the delicate slab above. From the ledge move
right 3m to move up the upper wall to the top.

BB 36 **Quarry Face** 9m   MS

BB 37 **The Tippler** 8m   MVS   4c

BB 38 **Lichen Groove** 6m   D

BB 39 **Diagonal** 6m   VD
A surprisingly awkward start distinguishes this last route of
interest.

Bowden Doors   GR NU 070325

Situation and access
Although situated fairly high (altitude 170m) on Belford Moor, this
south-west facing crag nestles in a sheltered position. Only its south
end (Main Wall area) is visible, a few hundred yards from the
B6349 Belford to Wooler road. The village of Belford lies just off the
A1 and from here the B6349 is followed towards Wooler for 3 miles.
Keep left when the road forks and on reaching the crest of the hill
find a gate on the right with the crag beyond. The long verge is just
wide enough to take cars carefully parked. The crag lies in the
grounds of North Lytham farm: access is no problem at the moment
and care should be taken to preserve this happy state.

Character
This deservedly popular crag consists of superb sandstone offering a
variety of steep climbing. Its south-westerly aspect ensures a

BB(23), The Vole, Back Bowden Doors

BD (1–20)

maximum amount of sunshine and because it is situated in the rain
shadow area of Cheviot it often remains dry here when raining
elsewhere. The crag runs in a straight broken line from south to
north and comprises a number of interesting vertical and
overhanging walls starting with Main Wall (the highest at 12m) and
culminating in the unique Wave Wall. Whilst many of the climbs
are treated as problems, and soloed, there are a number of routes
that can be protected and are climbed roped. In addition to the
routes described, there are innumerable short problems and girdles
which offer tremendous training.

The climbs
The routes are described from right to left. The first wall is reached
in a couple of minutes from the car.

BD 1 **Main Wall Eliminate** 14m E1 5b *
Start just left of the end of the wall to climb a line of flakes
and the wall above directly to the top.

BD 2 **Main Wall** 14m HVS 5b ***
A very good route up the centre of the first wall of the crag.
A shallow flake corner provides the start and is marked by
the presence of a crack above it at the top of the wall. Up the
corner to move out first right then climb back left to gain the
crack leading to the top.

BD 3 **The Viper** 14m E1 5c *
Start just right of the next route and climb to gain the
obvious rightward hand traverse. Follow this for 3m until a
steep move gains a thin crack. Up this to join the final crack
of Main Wall then break out right on good holds to the top.

BD 4 **Stretcher Wall** 12m HVS 5b *
A direct route of some interest starting at the left end of this

BD(1–20), Bowden Doors, Main Wall area

first wall and following a flake which leads to the small overhang. From the flake make a long reach to the horizontal break and continue directly above. Another long reach is made from where easier climbing reaches the top.

BD 5 **Deception Crack** 12m VD
A distinct slab separates this first wall from the next. Move up to gain cracks on the right and then follow a V chimney to the top.

BD 6 **Second Staircase** 12m D
Take the slabby break to finish up the short bulging chimney.

BD 7 **Y Front** 8m 5c
The red wall just left of Second Staircase provides a delicate problem.

BD 8 **Black and Tan** 12m S 4b
Move on to the top of the flake with difficulty then move diagonally right to crack. This leads with easier climbing to the top.

BD 9 **The Scoop** 12m HS 4c **
The scoop 5m left of Black and Tan provides a good route. The corner and scoop lead to a finish on good holds.

BD 10 **The Gauleiter** 12m E3 6a
Climb the rusty red-coloured wall direct past a horizontal crack at 2.5m.

BD 11 **Grovel Groove** 11m HVD **
This is the obvious Y-shaped feature in the centre of this second wall. Climb diagonally leftwards – much better than the name would suggest.

BD 12 **Goose Step**   9m   E3   6a
Begin by the pedestal and climb to a block. From here move
up and take the centre of the wall.

BD 13 **Flake Crack**   6m   S   *
Take the short slab near the left end of the wall to climb up
past the flake. Move right to finish.

BD 14 **Crater Maker**   9m   E3   5c
Begin 2m right of the corner and climb the curving fault to a
horizontal crack. The wall above using flakes leads to a hard
move to reach good finishing holds.

BD 15 **The Corner**   6m   VS   5a

The next little wall faces south.

BD 16 **Guard's Exit**   6m   VD
The niche in the wall just left of The Corner is gained
awkwardly by climbing a short crack. It is possible to finish
to the right or left.

BD 17 **Exhibition Crack**   6m   S   4c
Left of Guard's Exit is a crack starting about 3m off the
ground. Reaching it is the most difficult bit.

BD 18 **Red Nose**   8m   HVD
Climb the nose by starting up a shallow groove and continue
to finish right by Exhibition Crack.

BD 19 **Russet Groove**   9m   D   **
The distinct groove with the overhang at the top – good
holds but bulges midway.

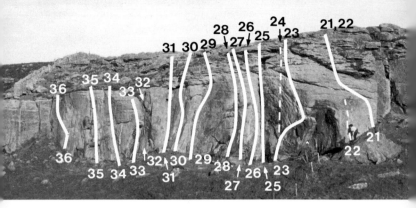

BD(21–36), Bowden Doors

BD 20 Overhanging Crack 9m E1 5c **

The exiting moves are the most insecure but good runners can be placed.

There is now an undistinguished recess then a short wall leading down to where a stone wall/fence (crossed by a stile) abuts against the crag. There are two climbs of merit on the short wall.

BD 21 Canada Dry 9m HVS 5a *

From the right end of the short wall (just left of a chimney) ascend utilizing a horizontal ledge to gain the leftward trending ramp. Continue along this until a step right enables the lip to be reached.

BD 22 Dog Eat Dog 5m 6b *

The left end of the short wall gives a steep fingery problem.

Just left of the above route the crag turns and becomes undercut. A stone wall/fence joins the crag and the usual start for the next route lies just to the left of this.

BD 23 **Canada Crack**   9m   HVS   5a   **
Start left of the stone wall/fence to arch right and gain a flake groove and follow it to the top. Alternatively an easier start can be made to the right.

BD 24 **Klondyke Wall**   9m   E1   5b   *
Start as for Canada Crack, but continue directly over the overhang and up the wall above on pockets.

BD 25 **Long Crack**   11m   HVS   5a

BD 26 **Jackdaw Crack**   9m   HVS   5b
The crack up the wall left of Long Crack leads to a move left into a wider crack.

BD 27 **Transformer**   9m   E2   6a   *
The short overhanging prow is climbed slightly from the right – a difficult problem.

BD 28 **Long John**   9m   S   4c
The nose to the left is split by an overhanging chimney. Climb it with an awkward move leading to good holds on the right.

The wall on the left holds two distinct leaning grooves.

BD 29 **First Leaning Groove**   9m   HVS   5a
This right-hand groove is the harder. Climb to a flake on the right and then make a hard finish up the left rib.

BD 30 **Second Leaning Groove**   8m   VS   5a
Up until an awkward move leads to better holds on the left.

BD 31 Blocked Chimney Corner 6m MVS 4c

BD 32 Nose Chimney 6m D
The deep chimney is usually used in descent.

BD 33 Brutally Handsome 6m E2 5c *
One of the classic problems – the name says it all. Climb the prow left of the chimney of Nose Crack until a vital hold over the roof enables a strenuous move to be made to the finishing holds. Finishing is the hardest bit!

BD 34 Scorpion 8m MVS 4c
The leftward leaning scoop gives a sting at its end.

BD 35 Crab Wall 8m S
Flake cracks are reached and then followed strenuously to better finishing holds.

BD 36 The Harvest Bug 8m E1 6a *
Start directly, then make a balance/friction traverse leftwards to gain holds that enable the top to be reached.

This wall terminates in a polished corner – interesting descent (VD in ascent) – with a slabby wall on the left containing three cracks.

BD 37 Triple Cracks 6m S 4c
Climb across the cracks from right to left.

On the left end of the wall is a second boundary wall running above and below the crag (take care not to damage this). The following climb starts directly above the wall.

BD 38 Wall Crack 6m MVS 4c

BD(33), Brutally Handsome, Bowden Doors

BD (36–53)

366

BD 39 **Castle Wall** 6m MS 4b *
Take the obvious line to trend right using the castellations at the top.

BD 40 **Sue** 8m S 4c
From the centre of the wall move diagonally right.

BD 41 **Castle Crack** 8m VD **
Climb direct – an excellent route.

BD 42 **Pitcher Wall** 9m HVS 5a
Climb the wall, some friable holds, to finish on the left.

BD 43 **Crescent Wall** 6m S 4b *
Take the ramp and use the crescent hold on the right to finish.

BD 44 **Runt** 9m VS 5a
Climb the cracks on the right edge of the next buttress.

BD 45 **Little Red Rooster** 9m E1 5b *
Take the flake finishing straight up the wall above.

BD 46 **Lorraine** 11m VS 5a ***
A fine classic. Take the layback flake to gain the upper horizontal break. Hand traverse left until a standing position can be gained in the break. Transfer from the ridiculous to the sublime and friction up the delicate slab above.

BD 47 **Don't Let Go** 9m E2 5c
The arete to the left is taken using a flake on the right to reach the overhang. Move left to a crack and then better holds.

BD(36–53), Bowden Doors

BD 48 **Slab Crack**   9m   E1   5b
The corner crack is a real grunt!

BD 49 **The Rajah**   11m   E5   6b   *
A steep start requiring a controlled dyno to ascend the wall
and reach the overhang. Move right 1.5m and take the
overhang at the break to climb the wall above. Hard and
serious.

BD 50 **Tiger's Wall**   11m   VS   5a   ***
Yet another brilliant route. Climb the wall, go over the
overhang and gain the prominent flake crack in the upper
half of the face.

BD 51 **Leo**   9m   E1   5b
The left arete of Tiger's Wall is climbed for 3m until a
rightward diagonal traverse utilizes three small flakes to
finish directly up the wall.

The wall ends in a recess containing two cracks – Red Crack
HS on the right and Black Crack VD to the left. The final
slabby wall offers the following two routes.

BD 52 **Banana Wall**   9m   MVS   4c   **
There is a ledge at 3m height and this is reached by the
diagonal leftward sloping flake. Continue to finish on
positive holds.

BD 53 **The Runnel**   9m   VS   5a
Gain the thin fluting with difficulty and follow it to the top.

The crag now breaks up for a short way until a long wall
contains an overhung shelf running its length.

BD(50), Tiger's Wall, Bowden Doors

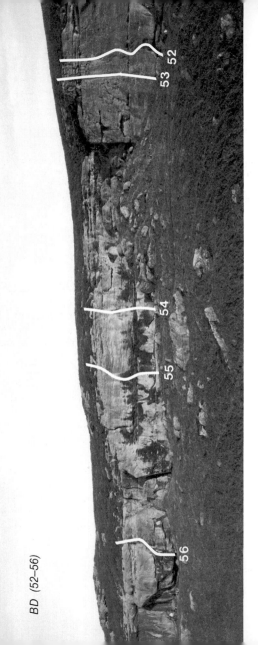

BD (52–56)

BD 54 Retreat   8m   E1   5b

Climb on to the shelf at 2.5m and take the shallow corner to a difficult exit. Finish right or left.

BD 55 Boomer   9m   E4   5c

The rock is better than it looks. Climb to the bulge and on to ascend directly to a basin at half-height. Go diagonally right to finish.

The next routes described take the buttress left of the recess containing a boulder.

BD 56 Giant's Ear   9m   VS   5a

Reach the flake crack from the left and follow it with some difficulty.

BD 57 Barbarian   11m   E5   6b   **

Climb the grossly overhanging flake crack until it stops. Small flakes enable the flutings above to be reached – by some. Best to make sure the finishing holds are sand-free before commencing.

From here on the wall is capped by a frozen wave of rock – Wave Wall is one of the most beautiful in Northern England.

BD 58 Poseidon Adventure   11m   E4   6a   ***

A brilliant climb breaking through the wave. Trend rightwards up the weakness (harder for the tall) to a short wall below the break. A hard move on a chicken head (crux for the short) enables a long reach to the break to be made. Traverse right until a high undercut in the wave enables one to stand in the break. Reach over – the wave is hollow at this point – and move slightly left to make the final pull over.

BD(52–56), Bowden Doors

BD (56–66)

BD 59 **The Wave**   12m   E5   6a   *
The distinctive flakes lead to a ledge. Continue with
difficulty to the horizontal break. Move right for a metre
then make hard moves over the wave. Move right and up the
wall to the top.

BD 60 **Rising Damp**   9m   E4   6b   ***
A savage upside-down flake leads left. Gain the flake and
follow it – very hard – until holds are reached and followed
to the top.

BD 61 **The Skate**   9m   HVS   5c
An undercut flake is used to surmount the overhang.

BD 62 **The Shiner**   9m   VS   5b

BD 63 **Bloody Nose**   8m   HS   4c   *

BD 64 **The Jury**   9m   E3   5c   *

BD 65 **The Trial**   9m   E2   5c   ***
A fingery start leads to a horizontal break. Move left and up
using an undercut then make a long reach to a hidden hold
and finish directly.

BD 66 **The Judge**   9m   E3   5c   *

Left again the wall diminishes and from here to the end there
are a number of enjoyable problems which provide a good
deal of interest – follow the chalk!

BD(56–66), Bowden Doors, Wave Wall area

CO-1 Fp-91

1
2
3
4
5
6

Causey Quarry   GR NZ 204560

Situation and access

The position of this old quarry, within easy reach of Newcastle, Sunderland, Durham *et al.*, justifies its inclusion here. It is sheltered, receives sunshine from mid-afternoon onwards and can offer a dry place to climb even in unfriendly weather. It is situated below the Causey Arch – the first railway bridge in the world – just off the A6076 Sunniside to Stanley road. It is reached by travelling towards Stanley when after 3 miles a large white pub, the Causey Arch, appears on the left. Turn right opposite this and follow the narrow road to the bottom of the dip. Parking is possible here. A stone track leads across a couple of concrete slab bridges and then a wooden footbridge. After the footbridge the crag lies just over to the right (5 minutes).

Character

Unfortunately the crag is rather dirty as an eroded top washes mud over the rock each time it rains. Additionally the quarried sandstone is relatively soft and cannot in any way compare in quality with the sandstone crags of Northumberland. Nevertheless there are a number of climbs of interest here and, with the overhangs above providing shelter, a natural, long, low-level traverse provides a non-serious and fun workout.

The climbs

The routes are described from left to right.

CQ 1   **Quarry Wall**   12m   VS   4c
   Ascending through the initial overhang is the most difficult.

CQ 2   **The Mangler**   18m   HVS   5a
   The pronounced crack splitting the wall. Probably the best route on the crag.

CQ(1–6), Causey Quarry, left half

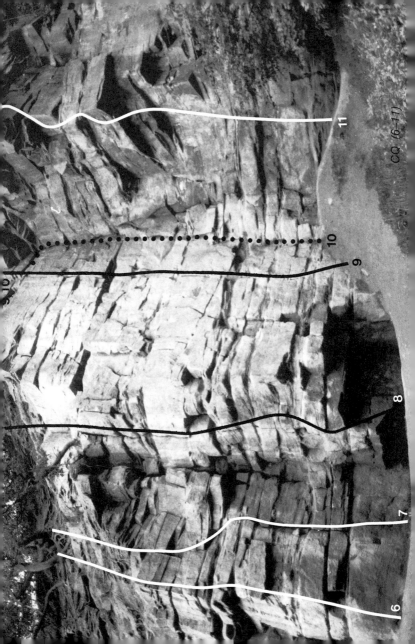

CQ 3 **The Dangler** 18m E2 5c
A crack splits the roof. Climb the wall through the overhang, then step left. Move back right to gain and follow a groove to the top.

CQ 4 **Hangover** 9m E1 5b

CQ 5 **Letterbox Wall** 9m E1 5b

CQ 6 **The Arete** 8m MS

CQ 7 **Wall Route 3** 9m S

CQ 8 **Causey Crack** 12m VS 4c

CQ 9 **Telstar Direct** 15m VS 4c

CQ 10 **Telstar Crack** 18m S

CQ 11 **Sandman** 14m E3 5c
The rock is very doubtful – a frightening test-piece.

Corby's Crag GR NU 127101

Situation and access

Lying immediately down below the B6341 and facing west, this is a very pleasant crag on which to climb. It is about 3½ miles east of the A697 (Morpeth to Wooler) and B6341 (Alnwick to Rothbury) crossroads. About half-way up a hill there is a tree on the left and space to park – there is a metalled parking space just a little further up the hill on the same side. Down below the lone tree a path falls

CQ(6–11), Causey Quarry, right half

CB (1–9)

directly to the left end of the crag and the most northerly buttress,
North Buttress (2 minutes).

Character
The crag comprises the North Buttress – which is the most
impressive – and the friendlier South Buttress (including the Upper
Middle Section) and Far South Buttress over to the right. The
North Buttress is steep and has a serious challenging air whilst the
others offer a variety of climbs suitable for most tastes.

The climbs
The routes are described from left to right. From the car the usual
point of arrival, if an immediate descent is taken, is the left end of
the North Buttress.

North Buttress

CB 1 **Sow**   9m   HS   4b

CB 2 **Crew**   9m   MVS   4c

CB 3 **Friday's Child**   14m   VS   4c

CB 4 **Ranadon**   15m   E2   5b   ***
       The clean central pillar is climbed to the break. Continue
       directly up the wall to the second break. Move left to gain
       the scoop and finish up this.

CB 5 **Audacity**   15m   HVS   5a   ***
       A line directly up the centre of this main wall. A flake crack
       leads to the overhang which is climbed slightly left. Climb
       the flutings directly above and move right to continue up to
       a corner. Trend left to finish up the slab.

CB(1–9), Corby's Crag, North Buttress

CB (10-23)

CB 6 **Plumbline** 11m MVS 4b

CB 7 **Easy Rider** 12m S

CB 8 **Black Wall** 12m VS 4c

CB 9 **Cake Walk** 12m D

> The crag deteriorates into a scruffy wall but up on a terrace above is another low clean wall. This is the Upper Middle Section which although short is of good rock.

Upper Middle Section

CB 10 **Hole-in-one** 9m MVS 4c
A hole by a flake 3m off the ground marks the route.

CB 11 **Sunshine Superman** 9m HVS 5a *
A diagonal crack connects two niches.

> The wall ends on the right with a steep bulging buttress – this is the start of the South Buttress.

South Buttress

CB 12 **Tiger Feet** 9m E1 5a
The overhanging arete.

CB 13 **Gibbon's Gambol** 12m E2 5c *
From the crack (Wonderland) hand traverse left and gain the slab with some difficulty.

CB 14 **Wonderland** 11m S
The wide rightward slanting crack.

CB(10–23), Corby's Crag, Upper Middle Section and right

CB 15 **Crossover**   17m   S

CB 16 **The Plonka**   12m   S   **
A popular route making an interesting diagonally leftward
ascent.

CB 17 **First Opportunity**   9m   HVD
Quite awkward.

CB 18 **Overunder**   9m   HS   4b   **
Follow the overlaps leftwards, then move on to a sloping
ledge and up the wall.

CB 19 **Temptation**   9m   VS   5a   **
After the overhang a long reach to a flake (care with the
rock) provides the key to the wall above.

CB 20 **Prediction**   9m   VS   5a

A few small broken walls lead to a wide gully – easy descent
– with the next distinct buttress on the right being Far South
Buttress.

Far South Buttress

CB 21 **Bluebird**   9m   E1   5c
The overhanging arete can be finished by pulling out either
left or right. Both are hard and precarious.

CB 22 **Misrepresentation**   9m   MVS   4c   **
The wall is climbed to the obvious corner flake and this is
followed to the top. A nice little route.

CB 23 **L.P.**   11m   VS   4c

CB(22), Misrepresentation, Corby's Crag

On the right a gully is choked by a holly-filled chimney and the next routes described take the clean end of the buttress right of this.

CB 24 **Little X** 12m   MVS   5a
The X is about 3m off the ground a few metres right of the holly. Gain it from the left and continue directly.

CB 25 **Mr Jones** 12m   D   *
A fence joins the end of the buttress and this route begins just to the left of this. Trend left and then right – many variations are possible but the climbing is worthwhile.

Crag Lough   GR NY 765679

Situation and access
Situated directly under Hadrian's Wall this crag, and its near neighbour Peel Crag, are perhaps the best known of the Northumberland crags. From the B6318 Military Road turn off north at the Once Brewed junction (Information Centre opposite) to park in the Steel Rigg car-park (free). Peel Crag is the first crag visible and beyond this can be seen Crag Lough, directly above the small lake of the same name. The footpath follows along Hadrian's Wall, first across the top of Peel Crag, to dip down before the beginning of the Crag Lough cliffs (15 minutes).

Character
The rocks reach 33m in height and there are many buttresses offering a variety of climbing – all inevitably vertical, however. The rock is Whin Sill which is a very hard (and dark) quartz dolerite. The rock is clean and remarkably compact but between the pillars that form the buttresses there is much vegetation. The climbing here

CL(4), Pinnacle Face, Crag Lough

CL(1–7), Crag Lough, Monolith Wall, Pinnacle Face, Hadrian's Buttress

can feel particularly awkward until one becomes familiar with the rock. A late afternoon or evening in summer is the best time to climb, for the crags face north-north-west at an altitude of 260m. Nevertheless, if the sun should cast its sparkle on the lough below, it is an endearing and absorbing place to climb.

The climbs
The routes are described from right to left. The first wall is quite short, but the climbing worthwhile.

CL 1 **West Corner** 11m S
Start at the foot of the buttress in a little corner. Ascend the corner and then pull left on to the face to move up and then right to a finishing crack.

CL 2 **Monolith Wall – Face Route**   14m   S
Start below and left of the monolith to gain it by a crack.
Sloping and polished holds lead leftwards and upwards.

CL 3 **Route 1**   17m   VS   5a

Pinnacle Face

CL 4 **Pinnacle Face**   12m   VS   4c   **
Starting from the left gain and climb the crack up the front
face of the pinnacle.

Hadrian's Buttress

CL 5 **Hadrian's Buttress**   15m   S   **
A climb of sustained interest. Go left to the edge and then
back right to the crack. Follow this until a move right leads
to two mantelshelves.

CL 6 **Hadrian's Chimney**   15m   S

CL 7 **Crescent Climb**   17m   S
Begin up the deep corner and follow this to a ledge. Step
right on to a slab and move across into a finishing chimney.

Tarzan Buttress

CL 8 **Tarzan**   24m   VD   *
Suitably named. Start in the deep chimney and climb the
right wall until a step across left above the chimney can be
made to a ledge below the rift. Climb this to the top of the
wall making a strenuous heave to another ledge. Take the
gap behind the pinnacle to finish rightwards.

CL (8–17)

Jezebel Buttress

CL 9 **Sinister Corner** 21m S *
Take the crack formed by the pillar to a top block. Step right
on to the wall and continue diagonally right. Up the corner
then left into another corner and climb to the top.

CL 10 **Jezebel Direct** 21m VS 4b *

CL 11 **Jezebel** 21m D

Dexter Buttress

CL 12 **Dexterity** 20m S

CL 13 **Why Not** 21m VS 5a

Broken Ash Buttress

CL 14 **Gargoyle** 18m E1 5b *
Climb the crack to the right of the corner to the overhangs
and move left under these. Make a difficult move into a
slight groove then step right to climb to the top.

CL 15 **Punch Line** 18m MVS 4b *
The corner direct to a hard finish.

CL 16 **Back Alley** 18m D
Escape left to a chimney.

CL 17 **Broken Ash Buttress** 24m VD
Climb up to gain a chimney which is followed to a large
ledge. Move right into a corner and follow it to the top.
Much better than first appearances suggest.

CL(8–17), Crag Lough, Tarzan Buttress, Broken Ash Buttress

CL (18–25)

Central Buttress

This is the highest buttress on Crag Lough, containing some fine climbs.

CL 18 **Crystal**   21m   HVS   5a
Start right of the foot of the buttress up an overhanging corner. The overhanging crack above is usually avoided by a step left until moves back right to regain the crack are feasible. Above this is a flake crack and at the top of this a ledge is traversed to the right until the top can be gained.

CL 19 **Grad's Groove**   21m   VS   4b
The groove with the chief difficulties at 3m.

CL 20 **Neglect**   23m   VS   5a   **
The wall is climbed to a chimney. Up this, by bridging, to a ledge and make a pull over the overhang on small holds.

CL 21 **Central Organ Pipe**   24m   HS
A strenuous thrutch – unless correct technique is used!

CL 22 **Bisector**   24m   HS   *
The crack and groove, passing large blocks at the top to finish leftwards.

CL 23 **Impossible Wall**   24m   E3   6a
A hard direct line up the wall.

CL 24 **Great Chimney**   24m/80ft   S   **
An excellent climb of some character. The chockstone is passed by swinging into space.

CL(18–25), Crag Lough, Central Buttress

CL 25 **Main Wall** 30m   S   ***

Takes the front face of the main pillar. Easy climbing leads
to a narrow sticking-out block foothold. Moving from a
standing position on this, up the cracked wall, is the crux.
Climb the wall to a horizontal break for the hands and then
up and right to a ledge on the edge. A groove leads into a
final chimney of some considerable interest. A ledge below
the top offers the wisest stance and belay for the final little
wall above which offers no problems.

There are a few more buttresses in the undergrowth to the
left and further worthwhile climbs – these are left
undescribed for those with the exploratory spirit.

Great Wanney   GR NY 935835

Situation and access

Although these crags, a line of interconnecting walls and buttresses,
are high on the moor (altitude 320m), access is quick and easy.
From the A696 (Newcastle to Otterburn road) turn left at
Knowesgate (there is a telephone box in a parking space on the
right). After a couple of miles the road forks – take the right fork
until just after the bottom of a large dip (forest on the left) there is a
large double Forestry Commission gate on the left. Park so as not to
block the gate and follow the track (no public right of way but there
have been no access problems to date) until it veers off to the right,
at which point another track continues directly down the break in
front. A section of crag is now plainly visible. At the end of this
break the crag is in full view and a path across the heather leads
directly to it (20 minutes). This approach is simple, dry and direct
but there are others: the crag can be approached from the back by
following the edge of the plantation that runs up from the middle of
Sweethope Lough. This way is shorter but suffers from the
prevalence of wet peat bogs.

Character
A wild and exposed crag which, because of its north-westerly aspect, does not see any sunshine until late afternoon. It often seems to rain here when it is fine elsewhere in the county. Nevertheless it is an important crag with a variety of fine climbing.

The climbs
The routes are described from left to right. A boundary wall clearly marks the left end of the crag. The few climbs left of this are accessible by means of a tiny swing gate abutting the crag itself.

GW 1 **Great Chimney** 12m VD

GW 2 **Absent Friend** 14m E5 6b
Follow the leftward impending crack (with an in situ peg and long sling near its top), utilizing holds (boreholes and ledges) on the right wall where necessary, to gain the left edge of the buttress. Climb the edge to the top.

GW 3 **Endless Flight** 15m E5 6a ***
Starts right of the boundary wall. Take the corner for 5m then traverse left to the edge. There is an in situ thread around the corner. Move steeply up – small nut runners can be placed with difficulty – until a pull right can be made on to the wall. Continue directly to the top. A fine route.

GW 4 **Boundary Corner** 14m VD

GW 5 **Hawk Slab** 14m HVS 5a
Finish on the right.

GW 6 **Idiot's Delight** 12m HS 4a ***
Start right of the rib and climb the scoop to the cave. Traverse left and move up the nose to make a delicate step up a slab on the rib. Continue directly to finish. A superb climb.

GW (1–24)

GW 7 **Great Wall**   15m   HVS   5b   ***

Takes the wall on the right. Start up the niche and use the crack until a horizontal traverse can be made to the right – easier than it looks from below. At the end of this make a long reach up to a crescent-shaped flake in the little corner. Climb this to reach a castellated ledge on the edge and then traverse right again around the corner. The short left-leaning overhung and undercut groove above forms the crux finish to this tremendous route.

GW 8 **Foxes Hole**   12m   D

The chimney to a terrace then move right to finish up another corner crack. Strenuous pulls!

GW 9 **Nose Chimney**   14m   VD

Easier to start left of the chimney, with a traverse into it.

GW 10 **The Last Retreat**   14m   E2   5c

Gain the arete from left or right and ascend the overhang and wall to a scoop. Up this and then climb the wall right of the arete.

GW 11 **Nosey Parker**   14m   E4   5c

The left wall of the gully. Start on the left to climb up to the break. Continue up to the rock scar which marks the former existence of a sickle-shaped flake. Go straight up to the top from here. Serious.

GW 12 **Central Gully East**   11m   D

GW 13 **Central Gully West**   14m   S

GW 14 **Northumberland Wall**   15m   E2   5b   ***

The groove overhangs and closes to continue as a crack in

GW(1–24), Great Wanney

the upper wall. Follow it to a horizontal break a little way
below the top. Move right using the break handhold then
pull straight up for the top. An excellent climb with good
and regular protection.

GW 15   **Main Wall**   12m   VD   **

GW 16   **The Brute**   8m   HVS   5a
The bulges are strenuous but protection good.

GW 17   **Enery's Ammer**   11m   E2   5b   *
Entering and leaving the scoop provides the interest.

GW 18   **Sweethorpe Crack**   11m   HS   4b

GW 19   **Squeezy Bill**   11m   HD
After the blocks a great deal of effort is required up the
chimney.

GW 20   **Rake's Crack**   12m   E1   5b   *
The groove and crack with the hardest moves at the end –
protection is good.

GW 21   **Rake's Arete**   15m   VD   *
The arete is taken for 8m until a traverse right leads to a
corner chimney. The obvious direct finish is E2 5c.

GW 22   **Jacob's Ladder**   12m   VD

GW 23   **Rake's Progress**   12m   VD   *
Climb to a ledge and up the overhanging crack to another
ledge. Continue to climb the chimney to the top.

GW 24   **Epitaph**   11m   MVS   4b
Start as for Rake's Progress until a traverse right can be
made to reach a crack above. Continue up this to the top.

GW(3), Endless Flight, Great Wanney

There are two lesser buttresses over to the right should one wish for more.

The Jack Rock GR NU 235044

Situation and access
Charmingly situated above the River Coquet, on its south bank, this
crag offers some excellent little routes of considerable character.
From the A1 take the B6345 to Felton. Proceed along this road until
just through Acklington village, where a road to the left is
signposted 'Warkworth'. After Morwick Hall is passed on the left
there is a bend with a narrow road off to the left (a broken sign on
the right now only reads '. . . WALK MILL'). Continue to the end of
this cul-de-sac, where there is ample parking space. The crag is
situated some 100 yards downstream but the best approach is to
walk back up the road (house now on right) until a little wooden
gate up the bank to the left gives access to a field. Continue along
the line of the fence (which is situated above the crag) until a gap in
the fence at the bottom corner of the field leads directly down to the
downstream end of the crag (6 minutes).

Character
This is another sandstone rock of considerable steepness. Although
it is only small – some 80m long and 15m high – for the most part
the bulging strata overhang the river and many will want to rope up
for these routes whatever their length. Fortunately the rock is good,
providing excellent hidden incuts, and the protection is fairly
frequent. Although the crag faces north it is of a sound, clean nature
and (on the right wall of Ancient Britain) sports prehistoric Cup and
Ring markings – the first recorded climb in Britain?

The climbs
Because the point of access described leads to the downstream end,
the routes will be related from this point, i.e. from left to right.

JR 1 **Spate Wall** 8m   HVS   5a
        Short but interesting, starting from the left to gain the arete.

JR(10), Pause and Ponder, The Jack Rock

JR (1–10)

2 3 4 5 6 7 8 9 10

JR 2 **Mouldy Corner**   9m   VS
The corner is hardest at the top.

JR 3 **Hanging Tree**   9m   HVS   5a   *
Climb the distinct corner directly to the top.

JR 4 **Salmon Leap**   14m   S
This can also be climbed direct with only a small increase in
standard.

JR 5 **Ancient Britain**   12m   E2   5b   ***
The overhanging corner capped by a roof is climbed directly
to an easier crack above. A fist jam helps to start but
however the groove is gained it proves problematical. Note
the ancient markings some 5m up the right wall of the
corner.

JR 6 **Devil's Wedge**   14m   VS   4c
Straight up the overhanging crack to continue up the steep
groove above.

JR 7 **High Board**   17m   S   **

JR 8 **Dry Fly Corner**   12m   MVS   4c

JR 9 **The Butcher**   18m   E2   5c   *
Start left of the groove in the face of the upstream buttress.
Up and hand traverse right into the groove and climb this to
move right into a cave. Move right then straight up just left
of the arete.

JR 10 **Pause and Ponder**   14m   MVS   4c   ***
Start just right of the arete to climb up for 5m before an
exposed traverse left can be taken using the handhold break

JR(1–10), The Jack Rock

KO (1–6)

to reach the arete. Move up delicately until better holds are reached and continue directly to the top. Good value.

Kyloe Crag (Collar Heugh) GR NU 040395

Situation and access
This south-west-facing crag is in a sheltered position near the edge of Kyloe Wood. From the A1 take the Fenwick turn-off along the B6353. Drive through West Kyloe (a church on the right marks the hamlet) until a road breaks off to the left (2 miles before Lowick). Follow this until just before the buildings immediately by the side of the road and a little way before the wood. There is a gate on the left and a track beyond: the end of the crag is just visible at this point. A wide verge provides the parking, but do not block the gateway. Follow the track through the fields to bear right beneath the foot of the crag. In summer the base is heavily brackened but due to the popularity of the climbing there is invariably a trodden and distinct path (10 minutes).

Character
A delightful crag consisting of a number of buttresses that offer a wide choice of routes of all grades. The rock is excellent and the sheltered sunny position means that this crag is eminently suitable for winter days.

The climbs
The routes are described from left to right. The first buttress easily seen just above the path is a clean wall with a deep chimney in its centre – this is known as Saint's Wall ('G' Buttress) and the climbs will be described from here. (There is another section of crag, known as the Quarry Face and partly hidden by the hillside, further left. This takes the form of a square-cut corner with a handful of routes not described here.)

KO(1–6), Kyloe Crag, Saint's Wall

Saint's Wall

KO 1 **Parity** 11m HS 4c

KO 2 **Trinity** 11m VS 4c **
The crack starts this route of increasing difficulty.

KO 3 **Temptation** 9m M

KO 4 **St Ivel** 11m MVS 4b
Gain and follow the groove to the ledge and proceed directly
up the wall above.

KO 5 **Litany** 11m HS 4b *
An undercut start leads up and right to the half-way ledge.
Take the thin crack in the overhang to finish.

KO 6 **Saint's Arete** 11m S 4b *
Move off the concrete shelter to climb the arete to the break.
Continue up the corner crack above.

Right again, and the nearest buttress to the path is
Overhanging ('F') Buttress: an imposing chunk of rock
consisting of two overhanging tiers.

KO 7 **Cloister Wall** 21m MVS 4c
The impending wall is climbed rightwards to the ledge.
Traverse left and then climb directly for 5m until a move left
gains a rightward slanting groove which is followed to the
top.

KO 8 **Birdlime Crack** 8m HVD

KO 9 **Coldstream Corner** 17m E1 5b **
1. 8m 4a. A crack and wall lead rightwards to the ledge.

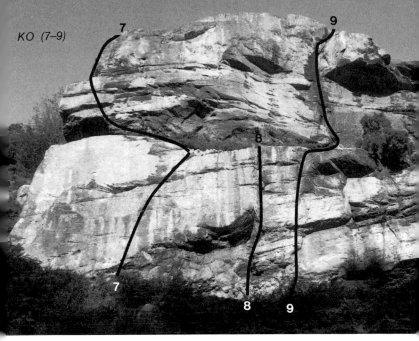

KO(7–9), Kyloe Crag, Overhanging ('F') Buttress

2. 9m 5b. The impending crack leads into the overhanging corner. Bold climbing leads to the top – excellent.

The next little crag is:

'E' Buttress

KO 10 **Hoglet** 9m VD
A groove on the left of the arete leads to a ledge. Continue just left of the arete.

KO (11–18)

A little further along, with trees at the base and a deep corner on the right, is:

'D' Buttress

KO 11 **Fawlty Towers**   11m   MVS   4c
Climb the arete to the ledge then finish directly up the nose on good holds.

KO 12 **Diminuendo**   12m   MS   4b
The crack leads to a large ledge. Move left and climb the wall.

There is a large clean attractive wall to the right of the recess. This is the start of 'C' Buttress – the most interesting section of crag.

'C' Buttress

KO 13 **Head Banger**   8m   E1   5c
An interesting, if short, wall problem.

KO 14 **The Pincer**   9m   E1   5a

KO 15 **Flake Crack**   11m   S   4a   ***
A magnificent climb for its length. Follow the flake crack and the wall above.

KO 16 **Tacitation**   9m   HVS   5b   ***
The delectable crack is gained after a strenuous and awkward start. Follow this directly to the top. The nose to the right is considerably undercut and gives two hard test-pieces.

KO(11–18), Kyloe Crag, 'C' and 'D' Buttresses

KO 17 **Prime Time** 9m E4 6b *

The overhanging recess (left of the next route) is climbed with some difficulty! Once the wall above is gained, the right edge is followed to the top.

KO 18 **Australia Crack** 12m E3 6a *

The overhanging nose is cut by a crack. Another brutish problem – gain the niche and move up until the crack can be reached and used. Finish directly up the slab.

The buttress now recedes into a tree-filled gully to re-emerge above 30m further on. The next section rapidly rears up and is still known as part of 'C' Buttress.

KO 19 **Christmas Tree Arete** 12m D **

Start just right of the nose and climb a crack, avoiding the overhang by moving left.

KO 20 **Gargarin's Groove** 12m HVS 5a *

Takes the prominent hanging groove through the bulge to the right of the nose.

KO 21 **First Born** 11m E4 6a

Climbs through the right end of the overhangs on to the steep wall above. Gain a groove from the right and then climb diagonally left to horizontal cracks to move into the corner of the overhang. Use an undercut to pull to a large hole and then flutings on the left.

The wide chimney, descent, separates the next buttress.

'B' Buttress

KO 22 **Deception Wall** 9m S 4c *

KO(19–21), Kyloe Crag, 'C' Buttress, right hand

KO 23 **Deception Crack**   11m   S   4b   **

KO 24 **Wilfred Prickles**   9m   VS   4c   *

KO 25 **Fakir's Slab**   9m   VD

KO(21–24), Kyloe Crag, 'C' and 'B' Buttresses

KO 26 **Slab and Wall Direct**   9m   HVS   5a   **

The end buttress is the smallest; nevertheless, it shouldn't be forgotten.

'A' Buttress

KO(25–26), Kyloe Crag, 'B' Buttress, right side

KO 27 **John's Wall** 9m S 4b

KO 28 **Chris's Arete** 9m S 4b

KO 29 **Twin Cracks** 9m S 4b
Use both cracks – or only one crack to make two routes!

KO (27–29)

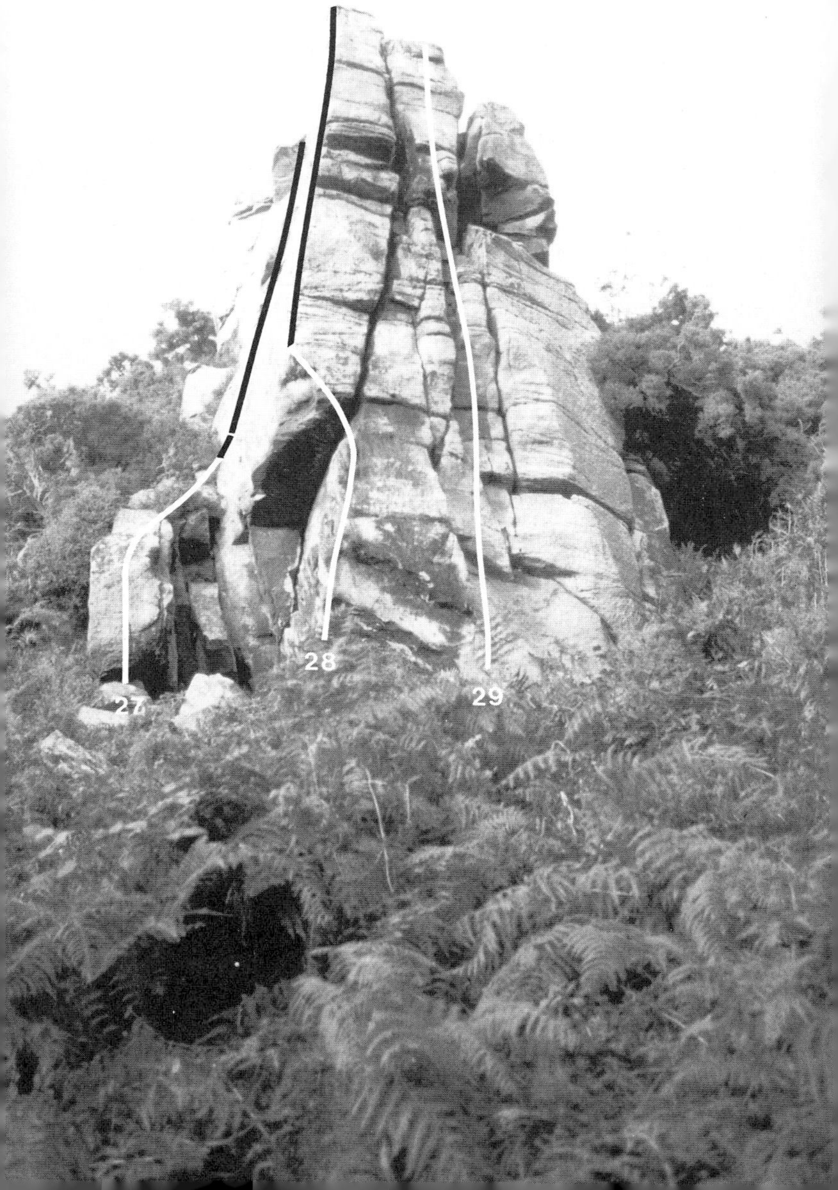

Kyloe-in-the-Wood (Dues Heugh)   GR NU 048385

Situation and access

Tucked away in a conifer forest, this absorbingly strenuous crag is
easy to reach. From the A1 take the Fenwick turn-off along the
B6353. Drive through West Kyloe (a church on the right marks the
hamlet) until a road breaks off to the left (2 miles before Lowick) to
skirt the west edge of Kyloe Wood. A farm is reached, followed by
the wood and then a wide entrance into the wood on the left. The
gate is locked and is marked 'Strictly Private'. Fortunately there are
no access problems but do not park in the entrance itself – the verge
on either side is adequate. Follow the track beyond the gate to a
junction (marked WS7) and bear right. Continue on this grassed
track until the line of crags appears on the left (15 minutes).

Character

The crag, an almost continuous wall of perfect sandstone, offers an
unparalleled selection of strenuous problems and climbs.
Charmingly situated in the wood and offering fine lines of great
interest, this is a small crag of impeccable character. The setting and
generally steep angle of the rock mean that climbing is seldom
interrupted by wet weather – most of the wall, apart from the very
top, remains dry. The many problem traverses, situated a few feet
off the ground, provide excellent sport and training. There are
routes to solo and routes to climb roped – all are distinguished.

The climbs

The routes are described from left to right. An isolated little buttress
may or may not be spotted before the continuous crag proper begins
but the first feature to note is a deep chimney – obviously square-cut
at the top. This is:

KW 1 Evendim Corner   9m   D

KO(27–29), Kyloe Crag, 'A' Buttress

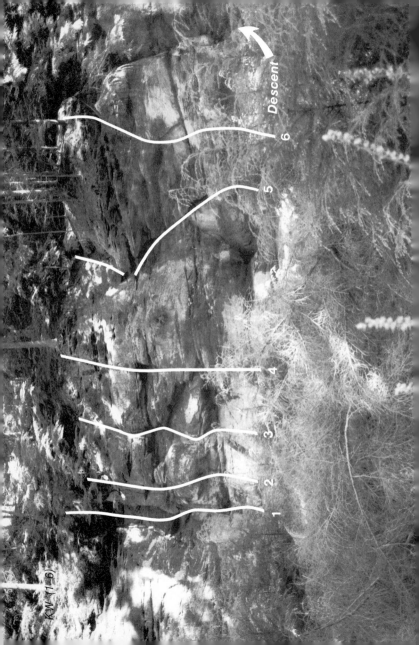

KW 2 **Aragorn** 9m S 4c

KW 3 **Frodo** 9m S 4c

KW 4 **Legolas** 9m HS 4c

KW 5 **The Hobbit** 9m VD
The leftward slanting corner leads to a wide crack.

KW 6 **Bilbo** 8m S 4b
The wall to a ledge and then a flake to a tree.

Right of this wall is a dark deep chimney – this provides the only easy descent for the central section of the crag.

KW 7 **Swan Crack** 12m MVS 4c
The left crack until half-height then traverse left and up a rib to the top.

KW 8 **Ostrich Crack** 11m VD

KW 9 **Marmoset** 11m MVS 4c
Use a flake on the right wall to gain flutings and the final scoop.

KW 10 **Red Rum** 12m E2 6a **
Start in a little corner groove and climb (various possibilities – none easy) to reach the edge of a small but obvious layaway flake. A long reach up and rightwards enables progress to be made directly up the wall.

Immediately right is a most noticeable feature – a large black coffin-shaped recess capped by an overhang.

KW(1–6), Kyloe-in-the-Wood

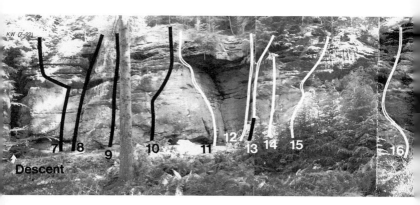

KW(7–22), Kyloe-in-the-Wood

KW 11 **The Elf**   12m   VS   4a   *

KW 12 **Right-hand Recess Crack**   9m   HVD   *

KW 13 **The Twitch**   6m   S   4c   *

KW 14 **Badfinger**   9m   E1   5c   **
The difficulty eases before the top, but it remains steep.

KW 15 **Bad Company**   9m   E2   5c   *
Gain the hanging rounded flake and trend right from this to
finish.

KW 16 **Monty Python's Flying Circus**   9m   E1   6a   **
A ramp, containing an upside-down layback crack, leads
diagonally leftwards to a niche. Above this is easy and
reaching it very interesting – a classic problem.

KW 17 **Crack of Gloom**   12m   MVS   4c   **

KW 18 **The Pearler**   12m   E3   6a   *
A crack goes half-way – climb it and the overhanging wall
until it is possible to traverse left to the arete. Ascend this to
finish.

KW 19 **Thin Finger Special**   12m   E1   5b   ***
The immaculate thin crack up the overhanging wall.

KW 20 **The Duffer**   8m   MVS   4c

KW 21 **Beorn**   10m   VS   5a

KW 22 **Beorn too Late**   10m   HVS   5b   *

The next large corner recess provides some good climbs.

KW (28-27)
27
26
25
24
23

KW 23 **The Flutings Direct**   12m   MVS   4c

KW 24 **Piccolo**   12m   VD   **
The chimney crack.

KW 25 **Verticality**   12m   HVS   5a   **
The right wall of the corner direct.

KW 26 **Zed Climb**   12m   MVS   4c   ***
Climb the slanting crack, moving left under the overhang
until it is possible to pull through the roof on good holds.

KW 27 **The Harp**   10m   VS   4c   ***
The wall is climbed until the obvious rightward hand
traverse is followed to the edge. Pulling on to and ascending
the slab to finish is delicate.

The crag now diminishes and recedes back into a corner – a
useful descent. Moving out right from the corner the wall
gains height and interest. The obvious and attractive
jamming crack is the next route described.

KW 28 **Primitive Crack**   9m   VD   ***
The approximate centre of the wall is split by this distinct
crack.

KW 29 **Dingly Dell**   10m   E1   5c   *
Take the wall about 2m right of Primitive Crack. Once the
break is reached the standard eases considerably and most
routes on this wall are treated as problems traversing off into
Primitive Crack along the break. Using the same start a
superior variation to this route is to step right reaching and
utilizing a small high pinch before a pocket hold in the break
can be gained.

KW(23–27), Kyloe-in-the-Wood

W (28—35)

KW 30 **Bobby Dazzler**   12m   E1   5c   *
The flutings.

KW 31 **Robber's Dog**   12m   E1   5c   *
The wall on pockets is the most interesting; an easier version
is the arete.

KW 32 **Piano**   15m   S   4c
The crack on the left of the corner is followed until a traverse
leads left and then up the flutings to the top.

KW 33 **Fluted Crack**   15m   S   4b

The wall going right from Fluted Crack has a green dank
appearance and it is advisable to ensure the holds are clean
before commencing on the next route.

KW 34 **High T**   14m   E3   6a   **
The T situated some 5m up makes this route easy to identify.
Despite appearances it is a splendid route with reasonable
protection. The final move is the hardest and is easier for the
tall. Start from the right and move up and across the
overhang to reach the T. Stand in this and move left to
pockets and protection below the finish.

KW 35 **The Crucifix**   12m   HVS   5a   ***
Climb the wall to the crucifix-shaped break and continue
strenuously up the crack to the top.

More routes remain and one of the best traverses continues
below. The best descent is also to the right round the end of
the crag.

KW(28–35), Kyloe-in-the-Wood

PC (1-5)

Peel Crag   GR NY 755677

Situation and access
Situated directly under Hadrian's Wall this crag, and its near
neighbour Crag Lough, are perhaps the best known of the
Northumberland crags. From the B6318 Military Road turn off
north at the Once Brewed junction (Information Centre opposite) to
park in the Steel Rigg car-park (free). The crag is now visible and
reached in a few minutes.

Character
The rocks reach a fair height by Northumberland standards (24m)
and consist of Whin Sill which is a very hard (and dark) quartz
dolerite. The rock is clean and remarkably compact but in between
the pillars that form the buttresses there is much vegetation. The
climbing here can feel particularly awkward until one becomes
familiar with the rock. A late afternoon or evening in summer is the
best time to climb for the crags face north-north-west at an altitude
of 260m.

The climbs
The routes are described from right to left.

Sunset Buttress

PC 1 **Twin Cracks**   18m   HVS   5a
   The first section is the most difficult.

PC 2 **Sunset**   23m   MS   ***
   Take the corner and move right to a ledge. The short wall to
   the large corner and continue up this to a platform. Trend
   left to finish.

PC 3 **Sunset Direct**   26m   VS   5a   *

PC(1–5), Peel Crag, Sunset Buttress and Blasphemy Wall

PC (5–14)

Blasphemy Wall

PC 4 **Overhanging Crack** 18m MVS 4b **
The wall and crack above.

PC 5 **Blasphemy Wall** 21m VS 5a
A tower leans against the wall – take the right edge of the
wall and move left to the top of the pinnacle. From the gap
move right and climb the centre of the wall until moves right
lead to the arete. Continue up this to the top.

Red Wall

PC 6 **Jester** 20m HVS 5a *

Central Wall

PC 7 **Ace of Spades** 20m HVS 5a
Take the right side of the broken pinnacle. From its top use
the crack in the centre of the wall until a move right enables
a direct ascent to be made to the top.

PC 8 **Certificate X** 21m E1 5a
Move from the cave to a ledge on the rib. Up the wall
moving left to a corner. Up this to a horizontal break and
traverse right to two ultra-thin cracks. At the top are holds
which enable a jug to be reached.

PC 9 **Rock Island Line** 21m E1 5b *

Tiger's Wall

This is the buttress immediately above the stone wall.

PC(5–14), Peel Crag, Blasphemy Wall, Red Wall, Central Wall and
Tiger's Wall

PC 10 **Trinity**   21m   S

PC 11 **Grooves**   21m   HS   4b   **
Near the top move right into the wide crack to finish.

PC 12 **Tiger's Chimney**   18m   VD

PC 13 **Tiger's Overhang**   18m   VS   4c

PC 14 **The Left Edge**   18m   VD
The left edge of the wall leads to the overhang – move over
and continue to gain and climb a crack to the top.

Although the crag continues this is the last area dealt with
here. Crag Lough is the next crag on the hill above the lough
(lake) beyond.

Ravensheugh Crag   GR NY 012988

Situation and access
This crag, situated a little way over from Simonside, has an air of
remoteness. However, access is quite reasonable on a good path and
track (which are also used to approach Simonside). Great Tosson is
the hamlet below the hill (reached in 3 miles from Rothbury) and,
from here, a picnic area sign marks the way. Follow the road
towards Lordenshaw until the Forestry Commission car-park/picnic
area appears on the right. Although the track leaving the right side
of the car-park eventually winds its way directly under Simonside
(the entrance gate is securely locked and vehicular access is
prohibited), it is better to take a direct line up through the forest to
join the track as it nears the plateau. To do this leave the left end
(looking in) of the car-park (this is the red trail on the Forestry
Commission sign) and follow a reasonable path up the break. After

a little way a burn appears on the left and shortly after this the Forestry track is gained. This soon emerges on to open hillside (the conifers above being felled in 1988). Ignore the various crags seen up to the left and follow the track contouring along the plateau until an open vista appears on the right and a crag appears on the left – this is Simonside north face. Stick with the track contouring the edge of the plateau but when it enters the forest again keep straight along on the path that skirts the right edge of the forest. After a short way the trees end and a fence and stile are crossed to continue directly to the edge of the plateau. Directly beneath is an easy grassy gully leading down to the end of the first steep little wall of the crag (1 hour).

Character
Never lofty, but high enough to make one carefully ponder the consequences of a fall, this is a unique climbing ground – both exciting and exacting. The crag continues in a series of walls but standing in front, for the most part, are two large pinnacles which, being detached from the walls behind, form buttresses in their own right. Most of the rock, perfectly rough sandstone giving excellent friction, overhangs or is at least vertical at the base with cracks and grooves forming the only breach in the defences. Consequently the climbing is both strenuous and delicate, requiring fitness and technique. The crag is exposed to the elements but the rock is clean and it catches the evening sunshine.

The climbs
The routes are described from left to right. To the left (east) of the grassy descent is a clean-cut little wall containing some worthwhile climbs.

RS 1 **Left Parallel Crack**   6m   VD

RS 2 **Central Parallel Crack**   6m   VD

RS (1–5)

RS 3 **Limbo**   6m   E1   5c
The overhanging wall.

RS 4 **Right Parallel Crack**   6m   VD

RS 5 **Little Idi**   6m   E1   5b
The wall is harder to start than it looks, and keeps its
interest all the way to the top.

The grassy gully now intervenes and the wall begins again to
the right, just before the First Pinnacle.

RS 6 **Plumbline**   9m   E4   5c   *
Climb the arete – a direct route giving excellent climbing.

RS 7 **Pendulum**   9m   HVS   4c   **
In the corner climb the left sloping crack. From its top make
a hard traverse left to the base of a deeper crack. Jam this to
the top.

RS 8 **Easter Grooves**   12m   E2   5b
Takes a series of grooves starting up a crack in the toe of the
nose. From the crack move right to climb the first groove
and then the steep groove above. Move left to a ledge on the
edge and continue with less difficulty to the top.

The First Pinnacle

RS 9 **Baluster Crack**   12m   E1   5b   **
A perfect exercise in jamming leads through the first bulge to
another and then a ledge. The crack above is somewhat
easier but the climbing remains consistently good.

RS(1–5), Ravensheugh Crag, Left Wall

RS (6–17)

Base of routes obscured

RS 10 **The Sandrider**   15m   E1   5b   ***

Take the crack until a move left leads to a ledge. Move right and take the crack through the bulge to continue on flat holds when the crack runs out. Take a right traverse and complete the route up the superb crack in the centre of the top wall of the pinnacle.

RS 11 **The Trouser Legs**   15m   E1   5b   ***

The classic – a magnificent problem giving sustained climbing and little or no protection. Start in a little corner left of the 'legs' and move up to make an awkward rightwards traverse to the bottom of the scoop. Climb the legs with interest to a rest below the overhang. Traverse right and gain a crack which leads to another crack and the top.

The Second Pinnacle

The obvious wide crack at the back is the easiest descent (Layback VD).

RS 12 **Honeymoon Crack**   14m   E4   6b   *

The central weakness up the front face of the Second Pinnacle. The great roof is climbed to a bulging crack and this in turn to a ledge. Traverse left to a wide crack which is followed to the top. The start is the most difficult and if climbed unassisted presents a formidable challenge.

RS 13 **Candle in the Wind**   21m   E3   6a   *

Another difficult start up the left line of flakes leads to an overhung ledge – gained with difficulty. Move along left and then climb up the arete with difficulty (a runner can be fixed over to the left in Honeymoon Crack).

RS(6–17), Ravensheugh Crag, First Pinnacle, Second Pinnacle, West Buttress

RS(13–19), Ravensheugh Crag, Second Pinnacle and West Buttress

RS 14 **Gates of Eden**   18m   E3   6a   *

The right parallel flakes are followed to a cave. Move across left to make a hard move on to the overhung ledge. From its right end make another hard move to gain the slab – follow this to the top.

RS 15 **The Crescent**   14m   S   **

The great curving slash gives a unique climb. Gain the crack and hand traverse it across the wall to the right until it is possible to pull into the rift. Progress through the rift and climb, on the far side, to the top.

There are a number of worthwhile climbs behind the
pinnacle (both on the back of the pinnacle itself and on the
facing wall) but they tend to be rather green compared with
the front face and are not described here. The following
routes are described on the next wall – West Buttress –
immediately right of the Second Pinnacle.

West Buttress

RS 16 **Ravensheugh Crack**   12m   HVS   5a   ***
The excellent crack is reached by climbing the wall via a

strenuous corner to gain the ledge below the crack. Gain the
crack and jam to the top.

RS 17 **Wild West Show**   15m   VS   5a   *
A corner is climbed to a break. Stomach traverse left to the
base of a handsome crack. Climb it to finish up the easier
angled slabs above.

RS 18 **Redskin**   11m   E1   5b   *
Climb directly to the bottom of the slab. Move on to the slab
and climb it directly to the top.

RS 19 **Moccasin Slab**   8m   HVS   5a   *
A bold route with no protection. Use the detached block
until a balance move enables a transfer on to the slab.
Straight to the top from here. (A distinct line goes out left
and is somewhat easier – Buckskin VS 4c.)

The rocks shrink from this point onwards, although they are
extensive, and no further routes are described here.

Sandy Crag   GR NY 968972

Situation and access
A high crag with a quarried-like appearance, visible from the B6341
Rothbury to Otterburn road. The Sandy Crags shown on the OS
L81 map are not the crag but merely a pile of boulders. On the way
from Rothbury a narrow masonry bridge is crossed (there is a drive
leading off to Midgy House from here but do not take this) before a
gate on the left, signed 'Midgy House'. Parking on the verge is
severely restricted. Walk up the track beyond the gate until opposite
the buildings. Go through a gate and cross the tiny wooden

RS(11), The Trouser Legs, Ravensheugh Crag

SC (1–3)

footbridge to the far side of Darden Burn. The path leads along then
directly up the shoulder. When the shoulder is crested (ignore the
rocks over to the left) the large mass of Sandy Crag can be seen (30
minutes). There is no right of way and during the grouse season the
gamekeeper may request that you do not approach the crag.

Character

The crag reaches a maximum height of 24m and holds some
impressive lines. It faces north-west and so takes the sun in late
afternoon but some of the climbs are rather lichenous. In addition,
the tops of some climbs are sandy; however, the excellence of the
lines more than makes up for these slight blemishes in character.

The climbs

The routes are described from right to left.

SC 1   **Sandy Crack**   24m   E2   5c   ***
> The classic crack of Northumberland. The line is obvious,
> taking the crack that cleaves the fine wall. Well protected
> with Friends. Start through the roof to gain the slab above.
> Continue up the crack, with increasing difficulty, to gain the
> horizontal break and a well-earned rest. Continue straight
> up the wall above, finishing just right of a scruffy crack.

SC 2   **The Vertical Vice**   20m   HVS   5a
> The chimney left of the wall gives the obvious line.

SC 3   **Angel Fingers**   20m   E1   5a   ***
> Another excellent route of sustained interest. Gain the thin
> crack from the left and then climb directly to the top. A
> climb requiring a variety of techniques.

SC 4   **Raven's Nest Chimney**   17m   HS   *

SC(1–3), Sandy Crag

SC (4–6)

SC 5 **Raven's Nest Crack**   17m   HVS   5a   *

SC 6 **Question Mark Crack**   17m   VS   4c
      Take the obvious flake – large Friends desirable.

Simonside   GR NZ 025988

Situation and access
This crag is the rugged north face of the summit bump of Simonside
Hill. It is one of the remoter crags in Northumberland and has a
real mountain feel to it. Even so access is quite reasonable following
a good path and track with the forest walk adding another
dimension to the climbing day. Great Tosson is the hamlet below
the hill (reached in 3 miles from Rothbury) and, from here, a picnic
area sign marks the way. Follow the road towards Lordenshaw until
the Forestry Commission car-park/picnic area on the right.
Although the track leaving the right side of the car-park eventually
winds its way directly under the crag (the entrance gate is securely
locked and vehicular access is prohibited) it is better to take a direct
line up through the forest to join the track as it nears the plateau. To
do this leave the left end (looking in) of the car-park (this is the red
trail on the Forestry Commission sign) and follow a reasonable path
up the break. After a little way a burn appears on the left and
shortly after this the Forestry track is gained. This soon emerges on
to open hillside (the conifers above being felled in 1988). The distant
crags seen from this point are *not* the north face of Simonside – to
reach this follow the track contouring along the plateau until an
open vista appears on the right and the crag proper appears on the
left. Stick with the track until a short path leads to the large picnic
boulder which is situated centrally below the crag (40 minutes).

SC(4–6), Sandy Crag

SS (1–14)

Character
The wild upland setting with remarkable views across the rolling countryside to the distant Cheviot hills makes this an appealing place to climb. But the day should be fair and the sun high in the sky for the crags lie at an altitude of 400m and face due north. Many of the routes follow cracks or corners but there is a fair choice, on sound rough sandstone. While there is particular emphasis on the lower and middle grades, there are some splendid harder routes.

The climbs
The routes are described from left to right. The first area to be dealt with here is the Boulder Face although some lesser buttresses can be found to the left again.

Boulder Face

SS 1 **Innominate Crack** 8m VD **
Follow the crack – sustained at the grade.

SS 2 **Flake Corner** 9m MVS 4c *

SS 3 **Flake Chimney** 11m VD *

SS 4 **Vibram Wall** 11m E1 5b **
The thin finger crack offers fine climbing. When it runs out a high hidden pocket eases the way.

SS 5 **Long Layback Crack** 11m VS 4c ***
A hard and testing classic. Straight up by whatever means you find most appropriate.

SS 6 **Over the Edge** 11m E3 5c
The wall and crack lead to the roof. Move right and gain a sloping ledge – a test-piece.

SS(1–14), Simonside, North Face

The next and largest buttress, extending furthest down the hillside, is 'A' Buttress. There is a half-way ledge which further identifies it.

'A' Buttress

SS 7 **Giant's Stair**   15m   *

SS 8 **Great Chimney**   17m   D

SS 9 **'A' Buttress Direct**   18m   VD
Start at the toe of the buttress.

SS 10 **Aeolian Wall**   11m   HVS   5a   *
Gain the ledge by traversing in from the right. After the wall a large flake is reached. Stand on it to move over the bulge. Ascend rightwards to the top.

SS 11 **Delicatessen**   11m   MVS   4b   *

SS 12 **Quartz Buttress**   12m   HVS   5a

The next toe down the hillside is:

'B' Buttress

SS 13 **'B' Buttress Chimney**   23m   S   *
An energetic climb not quite as hard as it looks. A finish up the upper wall can be taken via the scoop on the left (Cairn Scoop VD).

SS 14 **Cairn Wall**   21m   S   ***
The flake crack and then the steep wall above moving right. Continue right to a groove and follow this to the terrace. Continue up the crack above (Cairn Crack West VD).

The rocks now diminish and the descent track will be found over to the right.

Bibliography

Lancashire
LES AINSWORTH (ed.), *Rock Climbs in Lancashire and the North West*, Cicerone Press, 1983.
Helsby & Frodsham, Wayfarers' Club, (no date).

Yorkshire Gritstone and Limestone
Yorkshire Gritstone, a rock climber's guide, The Yorkshire Mountaineering Club, 1982.
Yorkshire Limestone, The Yorkshire Mountaineering Club, 1985.
Yorkshire Limestone & Gritstone Supplement, The Yorkshire Mountaineering Club, 1987.

North York Moors
Rock Climbs on the North York Moors, The Cleveland Mountaineering Club, Cordee, 1985.

Cumbria and Durham
S. G. WILSON and R. J. KENYON, *North of England*, Pointer Publications, 1980.

Northumberland
Northumberland, Northumbrian Mountaineering Club, 1979.
Northumberland New Climbs 1979–84, Northumbrian Mountaineering Club, 1984.